Birthright Reading

The At Series

Read in 24 Lessons

Linda Lee Gray Wilson

For Parents, Teachers, and Children

For students as young as 3 and as

old as 100

Linnie Rhodes Publishing

Venice Florida, USA

ISBN 9781735966137

Always make time to read to your child. One of my most successful students was a child who never went to preschool. The parents took their child to the library weekly.   That kindergarten student ended up winning a national writing contest. Reading is a lasting joy!

I am thankful to so many for being able to write this book. First, I must thank Charlotte F. Lockhart and her husband Jim for coming to my Montessori School in Ohio from Illinois to teach me and my parents phonics. Charlotte, a retired public-school principal, wrote a book, Discover Intensive Phonics for Yourself. It was Charlotte's personal touch that gave me confidence with sounding, sound-word blending and reading.

I also must thank my own parents, Mable and Lee Gray. My mother loved school so much she saved her books. She was born in 1914. One of her readers was The Beacon Second Reader by James H. Fassett and published by Ginn And Company in 1914. At the end of the book are twenty-six pages of Phonetic Tables. Any student that was behind was easily given reading help. This was a common practice until the whole-word movement omitted phonics.

To my dad, I am thankful for all of the doors he opened for me. He loved everything I wrote.

My final thanks is to people I never met. Thanks to Rudolph Flesch for his books, Why Johnny Can't Read and Why Johnny Still Can't Read. And finally, my gratitude goes to Julie Hay and Charles Wingo. They are the authors of what I believe was the last great public-school reading series, Reading With Phonics, published by J. B. Lippincott from 1948 to 1960.

And thanks to Larry for his book formatting.

The reading lessons are at the back of each book. Teach the lessons first by playing the sounding games and then easily read the stories. Do not guess at words and do not read the stories cold. Practice first!

Books 1-24 a-z letters & Dolch Words

Birthright Reading derives its origin from the Constitution. The first amendment proclaims free speech as an unalienable right. Freedom of speech expression is a direct gift from God. Children are born with the ability to make sounds. It is their God given right, a Birthright to be taught sounding.

The first sounds a baby makes are the five short vowel sounds, aaa, eee, iii, ooo, uuu. Babies are given an inborn sounding gift that prepares them for speaking and reading. According to Edward William Dolch, author of Problems in Reading (1948) and the word lists used today in reading, "No thoughtful person now disputes that children must learn the sounds which letters represent." (page 17)

When teaching Birthright Reading, always refer to the letters by their sounds not their names. Your students will soon be saying the letter sounds. After the first month, students will be able to blend sounds to form words. Sounding is the pathway to real reading.

My purpose in writing The Birthright **At** Series is to make reading as fast, easy and affordable

7

as possible. The At Series is a complete reading program. **Books 0 to 24** teach reading by sounding the **43 sounds**.

With Birthright Reading, a student can go from not reading at all to reading on the second-grade level. If your student is an older reader, it should be expected that he can easily go from failing to earning A's and B's in reading and all related subjects. Birthright Reading provides complete reading success.

The Dolch Pre-Primer and Primer word lists are required reading in most beginning reading programs. Dolch words are high-frequency usage words commonly spoken by children. E. W. Dolch knew readers needed to sound and read familiar words from their own speaking and listening vocabulary.

I found that once I taught my beginning readers how to sound the **40 Dolch Pre-Primer Words**, they easily sounded the **52 Dolch Primer Words**. If you can't sound a word, you lack reading growth potential.

Reading is not memorizing. Once you know the 43 sounds our 26 letters make, you can read almost anything. It's a fact that <u>87% of our</u> <u>syllables can be sounded</u>. In science, acceptable predictable patters are 50% or higher. Only, <u>13% of our words</u> <u>must be memorized</u>. **Sight Words (SW)** have letters that do not match their sounds.

Beginning readers do not need to know vowel and consonant special names. They just need to know how to sound individual and combined letters. All of the sounding basics needed for successful reading are taught in the 24 **At** Birthright readers.

According to E. W. Dolch, attacking new words is what sounding is all about. Library reading is introduced in Book 14 and goes to Book 24. Once a student masters the 43 sounds going to the library and selecting a book of interest is a satisfying reward. Independent reading is your final goal.

43 Speaking and Reading Sounds

20 Consonant Sounds

bcdfghjklmnpqrstvwxyz sometimes quiet k, b, g, w, l, t, gh knob, thumb, gnaw, wren, half, folks, castle, fight tion=shun action

ce,ci,cy=s ge,gi,gy=j q needs u c/k same

5 Short Vowels - at egg in on up

62% of all syllables have short vowel sounds

5 Long Vowels Say Their Name-a e i o u (w y)

Long Vowel Digraphs

Digraph – Two letters making one sound

ai-rain ay-day ea-eat ee-see ie-pie oa-boat oe-toe ow-low ue-blue

Silent e Vowels– name Eve like home June

y says long i (my) and long e (happy)

Small words ending in a vowel often say the long sound – no so go ho-ho Jo-Jo yo-yo he me we be she hi by my sky dry shy 5 Consonant Digraphs-chip ship this with why

3 R-Vowel Digraph Sounds- 1 car   2 for

3 her   sir   burn

3 Special Vowel Digraph Sounds

1 look   2 boo new   3 Paul saw

2 Vowel Diphthong Sounds

1 oink boy   2 out owl

Diphthong – Two letters making a

compound sound.

Blends – Two consonants slurred together.

Blends are not new sounds. slap, glad blue green clue drop flag plop stop trip sky

Once you know the 25 consonant sounds and the 18 vowel sounds and recognize

predictable patterns, reading is a breeze.

Dolch Pre-Primer & Primer Words Decoded

Pre-Primer Short Vowel Sounds a e i o u

and big can funny help in is it jump little up not red run yellow one(SW) said(SW) come(SW)

Primer Short Vowel Sounds a e i o u   all(SW) am at black but did get have(SW) into must on pretty ran that this under will want(SW) was(SW) well went what(SW)   with yes

Pre-Primer Long Vowel Sounds a e l o u w y

a away blue find funny go here where(SW) yellow I see three me we   my

Primer Long Vowel Sounds a e l o u w y

ate be came eat like no please pretty ride say she so there(SW) they(SW) white

Pre-Primer Consonant Digraph Sounds

sh ch wh th th - the three where

Primer Consonant Digraph Sounds   with

she **th**at **th**ere **th**is **wh**at **wh**ite **wh**o(SW)

Pre-Primer <u>R-Vowel</u> Sounds ar er ir or ur - f**or**

Primer <u>R-Vowel</u> Sounds **ar**e f**our** und**er**

Pre-Primer Vowel <u>Digraphs</u> oo, oo ew, au aw

t**o** tw**o** y**ou**   l**oo**k

Primer Vowel <u>Digraphs</u> – oo, oo ew, au aw

g**oo**d int**o** n**ew** s**oo**n d**o** t**oo**   s**aw**

Pre-Primer Vowel <u>Diphthong</u>   d**ow**n

Primer Vowel <u>Diphthongs</u> ou/ow oi.oy

out br**ow**n n**ow** **ou**r

Suggested Teaching Supplies

I have written four reading series. I love them all, but the **<u>At</u>** series is my favorite. Why? It is intended for use both at school and at home. For the cost of the **At** Series, and the added cost of teaching supplies, anyone can teach a child how to read.

My neighbor used the At series over the summer and taught her six-year-old grandson how to read in three months. He could not read when she started the lessons. When he returned to school, he was tested on the second-grade reading level.

My niece called me up in a panic several years ago. Her public-school was threating to fail her second-grader and put her in a special class. My niece removed her daughter from school for three months. She called me almost daily. I sent her all of the materials and supplies I am sharing with you. After three months, her daughter could go to the library and independently read.

My niece returned her daughter to public-school. The school tested her. She was on grade-level. There was no more talk of special classes or grade-level failure.

Reading on the second-grade level was a common occurrence in my public-school kindergarten class. Like all teachers, I was required to teach reading with the curriculum provided. What I did to make any curriculum work was to decode the vocabulary and spelling words for the children and teach them how to sound.

One year, when teaching second grade, I took all the students that failed the first- grade end-of-the-year reading test. Again, all I did was to teach them how to sound their vocabulary and spelling words. At the end of the year, they all passed to third grade. Several students scored in the gifted range on the standardized reading test.

How was I, my neighbor and my niece so successful? Prior to our sounding-reading we played the games I have suggested and used the simple supplies I have listed.

I sent my neighbor and my niece a mystery bag, Aa, Bb, Cc, upper-and-lower case letters, a chalkboard, eraser, index cards and a pencil box. These are the same supplies you will be using to teach any Birthright reading series. We learn through games and our five senses.

1   A **Pencil Box** - You will need a box to put the new words in after each lesson.

2   **Word Wall** at the child's eye level.   Put new words up in a clear open space.

3   **Index Cards** – New words and letters are at the end of each lesson. Teach the words and letter-sounds at the back of each reader prior to teaching and reading the story.

4   **Fat pencils, a pencil sharpener, a fat eraser, and dark markers or dark crayons**. Follow the printing guide arrows and numbers for correct printing. Always print from top down.

5   **A Mystery Bag** – In the Montessori classroom, a mystery bag is used for the child to touch and feel new letters. Any small bag will do, even a paper bag. Developing the sense of touch is very

important to the young child. It teaches focus and defined movement.

6 **Lowercase abc Letters** – You can find lowercase letters at most department stores or dollar stores. You can also buy uppercase letters. They will be used when introduced. **98% of all our reading is done with lowercase letters.**

7 **A chalkboard, chalk, and an eraser.**

8 **A box of eight fat crayons is best**.

9 A bottle of **Elmer's Glue All** - Put a small stream of glue or small dots of glue over the letter and let it dry overnight. **Touchable Letters** are training for printing and sounding. Touch each letter with clean dry hands using the pointer and middle fingers.

Suggested Teaching Games

Book 0 teaches the 25 letter sounds. We have 26 letters, but since **c** and **k** say the same sound, we only have 25 sounds. The dots under each page are for the child to touch and say the sound.   Book 0 teaches 20 consonant and 5 short vowel sounds.

Included in Book 0, is a page of the lowercase abc's. Touch the dots under each letter and **sing the abc song**. You will sing the song not by singing the name of each letter. **You will sing the sounds**. Soon, singing the sounds will become second nature. Do this each day.

Book 1 You are teaching the short vowel sound of **a** in **a**t, the consonant **t** sound and the word **at**. Make three cards a, t, at. They go in the **Word Box**. Make a second set to put on the **Word Wall**.

Prior to putting the three cards on the wall play a game of **Knock-Knock**. Turn all six cards upside down. Put them in a square in front of the child. Say, "Knock-Knock" on two cards and turn them over. Did you find a match? Say the sound and turn them back over if you did not match. If you did find a match, say the sound and keep the cards. Take turns playing Knock-Knock.   Play Knock-Knock with each new lesson. It teaches letter sounds, sounding, and new words. My students played it daily.

Play **Tic-Tac-Toe** three in a row **Bingo**. After Book 1 you will have more than 9 word and letter cards. You will need 9 cards to play. Lay any 9 different cards face up. To play, you need three rows of three in a row.   The Bingo caller calls any random letter sound or word that has been taught. If you have a word or letter that has been called, put a marker on top. The caller says the sounds and words. Three in a row, wins.

I had a professor who suggested we save small lids. I love saving them.   Lids make excellent markers for playing sound games.

Use the chalkboard. Model making the new letters on the chalk board. Let the child make

the new letters and words. Say the sounds. Sound the letters and blend the words. The most popular day in my room was Monday, student chalkboard day.

Put your letters for the current lesson in the **mystery-bag**. Have the child feel the letters in the bag. The child says the sound of one of the letters and pulls it out of the bag. Did the sound match the letter? Yes!

Go hunting for letter sounds. Take a letter from the new lesson. Go around the room and find objects that match the letter sound. When hunting for the **t** sound, you might find a **t t** table, some **t t** tape, a **t t** tie, or touch your **t t** tooth, and your **t t** tongue.

In the Montessori classroom, we had **sound boxes** with each sound. I still have my sound boxes. You can have one sound box where the child can put objects with the current letter or letter sounds and then change it out with any new sounds. Sound boxes and sound games make reading fun.

In the classroom, Friday was Mystery bag day. Students were allowed to bring objects from home that fit in their small mystery bag. They said the sound and got to sit in the **sound chair** with their mystery bag objects.

Each Birthright lesson has a space for printing the new letters and words. Have the child use a fat pencil for printing and sounding the new lesson. The numbers and arrows teach the **printing sequence**.

We hold a pencil with our thumb and pointer finger. The pencil rests on the bent middle finger. With the **At** series, you are not teaching printing, but you are introducing it. We are laying a foundation for proper printing. A young child does not need to be able to print to learn how to read.

You will love introducing printing with sounding. Children love learning how to properly use a pencil. Encourage pencil use and pencil activities with your student.

Play **I Spy a Letter and the Color Is**…. On a plain sheet of paper print the lowercase abc's. Use the whole paper and space the letters an equal distance apart. With a pencil, draw a circle around each letter.

Have your student color around each letter. When the coloring is complete, play the game. Say, "I spy a letter and the color is." The talker names the color. Take turns naming the color and guessing the letters by saying the letter sounds.   We played this game daily while getting ready to go home from school. A student was picked daily to be in charge of the game.

Games and movement make learning to read easy. **After you have played the games, it is time to read the story**. **The student will touch the dots under the story**. After reading the story, buddy read. Two students take turns reading each page. We did **buddy reading** daily. Make sure to do the printing and sounding on the last pages.

If you are sharing a book, you can have the student print on a separate sheet of paper. All the beginning printer needs is a single line tor printing. **Use the examples in the book as a model for printing**.

Play the matching game. With the abc letters you bought at the store, have the child match the letters to the word card. Make sure when you print the word cards your letters are spaced so your student can lay letters on top.

We matched letters to words two days in the classroom. After the student matched the letters, he raised this hand. A teacher helper came and listened to the student sound the letters then read the word.

After a few lessons, you will have enough words to **make a sentence**. This is a very important lesson. The young reader needs to be able to make a sentence and read the sentence he has made.

Here are sentence examples from Book 2. Nan ran. Ann ran. Tan rat ran. Make sure your sentences start with a capital and end with a period, question mark or exclamation point. **Add end mark cards to the word box**.

It takes about four weeks for a child to be able to sound-blend words. A favorite memory of mine is when young Tiffany said, "But Mrs. Wilson, I can't read." I said, "Yes you can, Tiffany. You just don't know it yet." In three weeks, Tiffany was reading.

In conclusion, teach each lesson by playing Knock-Knock, I Spy, Bingo, Mystery Bag,

Sound Hunt, Touching the Letters and Sounding, Chalkboard and Pencil Printing, Matching, Buddy Reading, and Sentence Making. In the classroom, we usually learned the new lesson in three-to-four days.

Friday was Fun Friday. We, the entire classroom, read our new story to a neighbor or to the office staff. A child would lead the class by saying, "Ready, Begin!" The students would read a sentence together. The leader said, "Ready, Begin" again, and the students would read the next sentence. The **choral reading** was a grand experience for everyone.

On Thursday's, I listened to each individual student read the story. **I typed the story and listened to the student read without pictures**. I gave them a percent grade and sent the graded paper home. All the students got A's.

We also had spelling tests and story-writing tests. When I gave the spelling tests, I exaggerated the letter sounds. I said, "Spell **<u>rat</u>**. The sounds are **r   a   t**." It works best if you don't repeat instructions. You are teaching ear-training. Say sounds boldly.

When writing stories or sentences sound. Say, "The sentence is, **I see a rat**. Start with a capital letter and print **I**. Use a finger space and print **see, (s e e)**. Use another finger space and print **a**. Use a finger space and print **rat, (r a t)**. End the sentence with a period."

In the Montessori classroom, we taught the **Three Period Lesson**. Here is how it works. You say to the child, "This is **a**." You say the short sound. Then, you look at the child and say, "Where is **a**?" The child points to the **a**. Finally, you touch the **a** and say, "What is this?" The child should say the short sound of **a**.

Another important three-part lesson is **Beginning, Middle and End**. The young reader must hear a first sound, the middle sound and the last sound of words. For example, in the word **c a t**, ask the child what sound comes last? What sound comes first? What sound comes second?

You can clap as you say the sounds or tap a table to help a child hear three sounds. Ear training is an extremely important lesson. It teaches focus, sound understanding, and sound placement.

The Birthright lesson outline includes spelling words and sentence writing. Spelling and writing are optional activities. Spelling and writing build reading skills.

Suggested Sounding Spelling

Only words with clear sounds have been included in the lessons. The number of words used is up to the instructor. I started out with 5 and worded up to 20 plus a short sentence.

On Friday, I sent spelling words home with the homework packet. Homework was a district requirement. Daily the students buddy spelled the weekly words. **Spelling words make great word wall words**.

Book 1 a, A, t, T, at

Book 2 ran, Nan, tan, ant, Ann, rat,

r, R, n, N, to   <u>Ann ran to rat</u>.

Book 3 <u>An ant ran</u>. <u>I ran to a rat</u>.

Book 4 c, C, cat, can, go, (the)

<u>Can cat go to Ann</u>?

Book 5 m, M, d, D mad, dad, Matt,

mat, Dan, man, add, Cam. ram,

<u>Can a mad ram add</u>?

Book 6 p, P, s, S, no, so, Pam, Sam, Pat, sat, and, sand, as, pass, cap, tap, map, nap, rap, sap, sad, <u>Pam and Sam sat at a mat</u>.

Book 7 i, I , it, is, in, did, do, into, Sid, Sis, Sig miss, dip, rip, sip, tip, pit, sit, mitt, tin, inn, pin

<u>Miss Sis is in the pit</u>.

Book 8 h, H, hand, hat. ham, hint, hip, Hap, hit, hiss, had, him, his <u>Can Hap hit it to him</u>?

Book 9 b, B, g, G this, that, big, bag, bat, bin, bib, bit, bam, gab, grab, sing, singing,

ding, dinging, ring, ringing, pig, rig, Tig

<u>Is that big pig singing</u>?

Book 10 l, L, k, K, ck, black, all, ball, hall, tall, mall, call, Mack, back, pack, sack, rack, lack, Dick, pick, lick, Rick, sick, hid, bid, rid, kick, kid, kiss, kit, Kim, Kip, king, packing, Lin, kicking, backing, lacking, picking, licking

Rick hid his black backpack.

Book 11 j, J, u, U but, must, up, jump, pup, pump, lump, bump, hump, dump, Jill, jig, jam, Jack, Jim, Jan, jug, gum, Jip, Pip, luck, buck, duck, dug, lug, bug, hug, mug, rug, cup, mutt, nut, rut, cut, tub, dust, fun, run, sun, Jack and Jill ran up the hill.

Book 12 y, Y, v, V say, may, pay, day, Ray, hay, bay, Fay, Jay, Kay, van, Val, Vic, yam, yuck, yak, yip, Jay and Kay ran to the van.

Book 13 e, E, f, F, red, yes, Bev, get, help, fed, bed, Ted, Jed, Ned, best, test, rest, nest, deck. pick, peck, egg, leg, beg, Meg, Jen, Ken, pet, net, yet, met, vet, set, let, Jell, fell, tell, fit, fig, yell, Tess, Tell Bev that Jeff fell.

Book 14 w, W, will, well, went, with, Wes, wig, web, wag, wing, wet, wed, way, wam,

west, Wes and Will went to the wet duck.

Book 15 o, O, not, on, mom, Tom, rock, sock, dock, clock, lock, clock, hot, lot, got, tot, dot, rot, God, Rod, nod, log, hog, dog, frog, hop, top, stop, pop, mop, cop, drop, tick-tock, Don, Ron, Jon, Bob, sob, off,

28

Bob and Rob got a tall dog.

Book 16 sh, ch, wh, th, th, she, chip, ship, with, the, chop, shop, whip, this, that, when, think, thank, Chuck, chill, She is on the ship.

Book 17 are, car, jar, far, bar, par, star, hard, park, yarn, barn, or, for, born, under, sister, her, bird, sir, burn, turn, The car is at the park.

Book 18 ate, Kate, lake, take, make, Jake, rake, bake, snake, wake, cake, play, way, away, say, day   Kate went away to a lake.

Book 19 he, me, she, we, be, see, Lee, Dee, bee, three, tree, bee, free, green, feed, meet, feet, sweet, weed, seed, need

He will meet me at the green tree.

Book 20 like, ride, find, kind, white, bike, my, by, hike, bite, hide, side, slide, tide, Mike, line, mile, file, tile, while, awhile, Nile, pile,

Mike will ride his bike to the hike.

Book 21 go, no, so, ho-ho, yo-yo, Jo-Jo, yell, yellow, glow, blow, slow, mow, low, glow

Can my yellow yo-yo glow?

Book 22 soon, boo, to, into, blue, Sue, glue, too, do, moon, noon, spoon, balloon, good, cook, book, hook, look, pool, cool,

Sue forgot her good cook book.

Book 23 out shout, pout, owl, boy, toy, Floyd, flower, shower, power, tower, oil, soil, boil,

Shout it out! Do not pout!

Book 24 q, Q, x, X, z, Z, quack, queen, fox, fax, fix, mix, Dix, six, box, ox, zip, zipper, Oz, Zebra, zoo, quilt, quit, quick,

Queen Dix went to Zebra Zoo.

She saw six ducks.

She fixed lunch for all six ducks.

Suggested Three Sentence Stories

Like spelling, three sentence stories are not required. They teach reading, spelling and writing. Three sentence stories show what happened first, next, last, or beginning, middle and end.

Three sentence stories also easily teach comprehension. Phonics students learn logic, analysis and reasoning. They think about what they are reading and writing.

Three sentence stories can also be used for handwriting lessons. Talk about the three letter shapes, tall, small, and tail letters. Tall and small letters sit on the baseline and never go below it. Tail letters go below the baseline. The baseline is the bottom line.

Tall letters b d f h k l

Small letters a c e i m n o r s u v w x z

Tail letters g j p q y

All capital letters are tall letters.

ABCDEFGHIJKLMNOPQRSTUVWXYZ

If you are teaching formal handwriting, the lines have names too.

Headline _____ Touch your head.

Midline _ _ _ _ _ _ _ _ _ _ _ _ Touch your waist.

Baseline _____ Touch your feet.

Children age five and under do not need to be taught formal printing. It is better to use no lines or only the baseline for a young child.

31

Printing between lines takes focus and fine motor control.

Here is a progression for teaching printing on the baseline. Follow the printing letter models at the end of each **A**t reader.

1 First, make letters in the air with the pointer finger. Knowing the strokes of each letter is the key to proper printing.
2 Touch the glue-dot letters.
3 Print the letter or letters on a chalkboard. Do each stroke slowly.
4 Print the letters and words on the baseline in the **At** reader.

Books 1 & 2 Ann ran. Nan ran. Rat ran.

Book 3 A rat ran. An ant ran. I ran to Ann.

Book 4 I can go. Can cat go? No! No! No!

Book 5 Dan is at a mat. Matt is at a mat.

I am at a mat too.

Book 6 Pam sat. Pam sat at the sand.

Pam pats a cat at the sand.

Book 7 Sis is at the inn. Sis ran into Sid.

Sis and Sid swim at the inn.

Book 8 I have a ham in my hand. MMmm!

Hap can have ham, too.

Book 9 Bud is big. Bud has a big hat.

Big Bud can sing in his big hat.

Book 10 Rick is sick. I can go to Bill.

Bill ran to sick Rick, my tan cat.

Book 11 Jack and Jill ran up a hill. Jump,

Jack and Jill. Run and jump in the sun.

Book 12 It is a sunny day. Kay ran to the bay.
Can Kay play at the bay all day?

Book 13 Jeff fell. Ned can ring his bell.

Peg ran to help Jeff.

Book 14 Wes wins a wagon. Wes gets in it.

Go, wagon, go!

Book 15 Bob has a frog. His frog can hop.

Bob has to run to get his frog.

Book 16 Can she chop it? Yes, she can.

Meg can chop the log.

Book 17 Art has a cart. Sis has a cart, too.

His cart is red, and so is hers.

Book 18 Who can play? Can Sam play?

Sam and I can play today.

Book 19 Can he see me? We see him.

Sam and I see Lee.

Book 20 I like it. It is my white bike

I will ride it on my bike hike.

Book 21 I see June. June is blue.

June can not find her blue hat.

Book 22 Look, I see Tim. Do you see Tim?

Good, we can play today.

Book 23 Now, can we go down town?

We will see Ed. Ed has a brown dog.

Book 24 I see Queen Zal. I can help her.

I can fix her tan mitt.

Book 0

a b c

O O O

Touch the dots!

Say the sounds!

1.. a...a...apple

2. b...b...bat

3. c... c...cat

4. d...d...dog

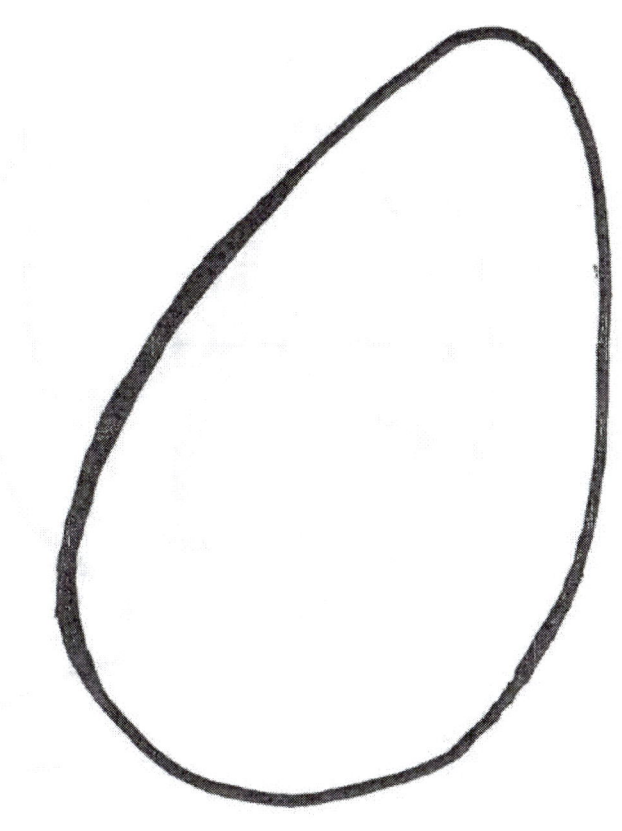

5. e...e...egg

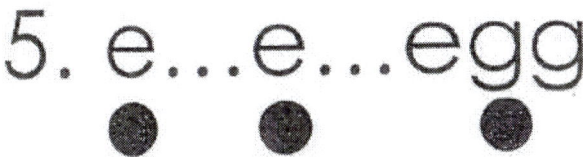

6. f...f...fan

7. g...g...gum

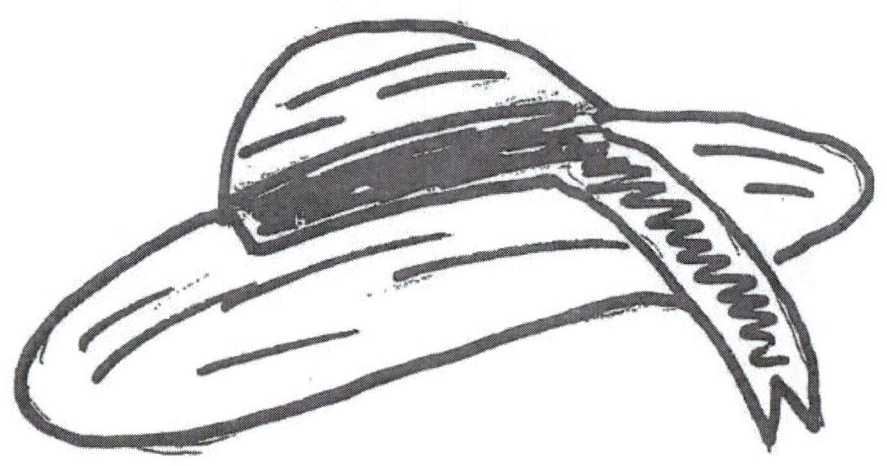

8. h...h...hat

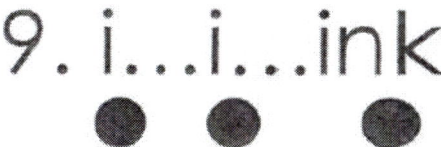

9. i...i...ink

10. j...j...jam

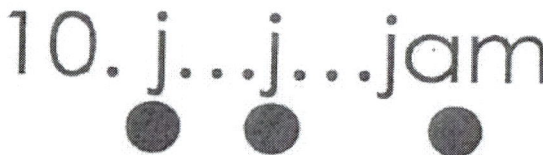

11. k...k...king

12. l...l...log

13. m...m...mop

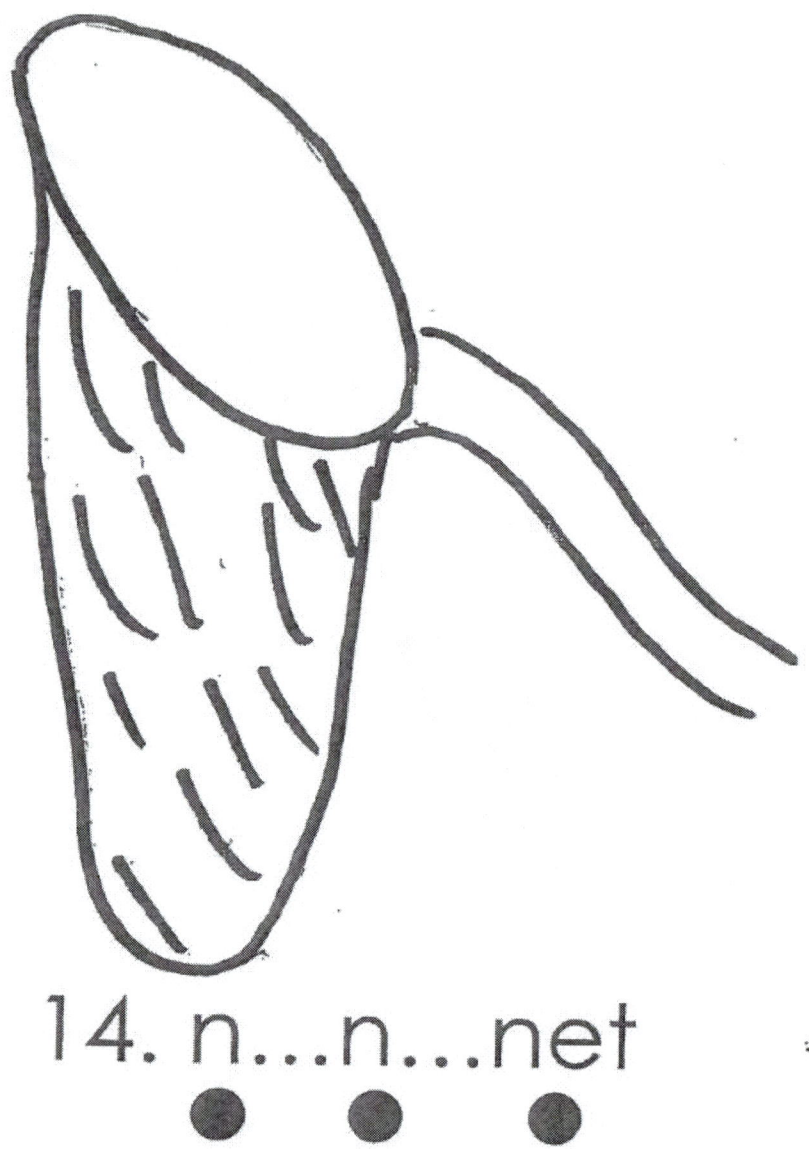

14. n...n...net

● ● ●

15. o...o...ox

16. p...p...pig

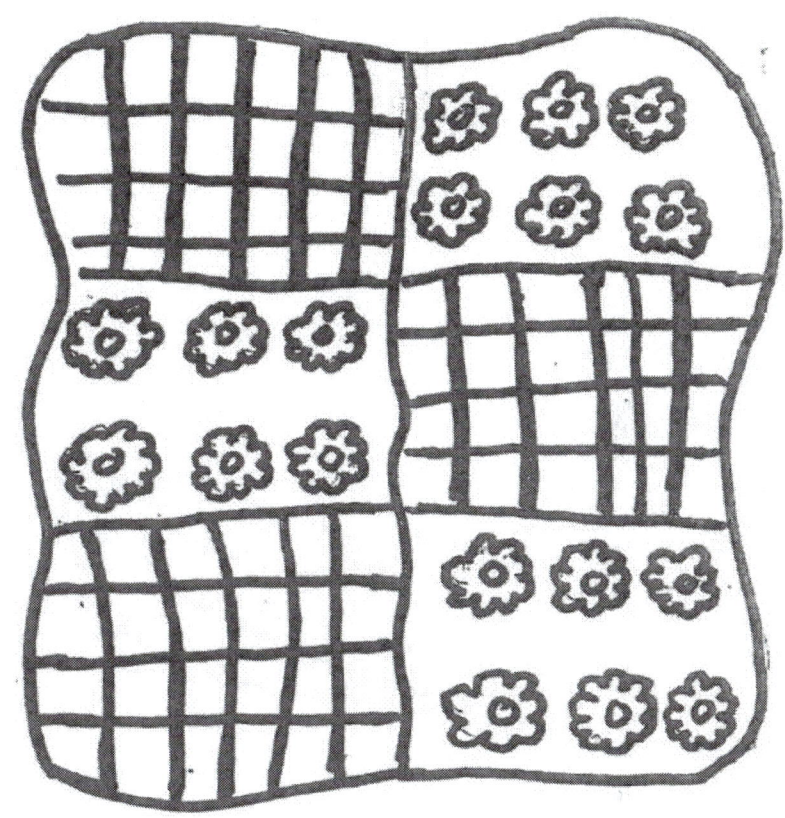

17. q...q...quilt

18. r...r...rat

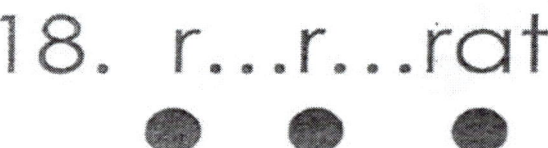

19. s...s...sun

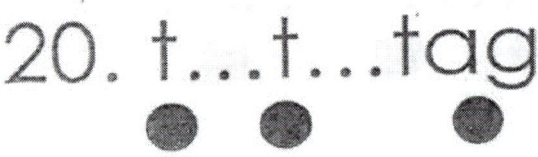

20. t...t...tag

21. u..u..umbrella

22. v...v...van

23. w..w..wagon

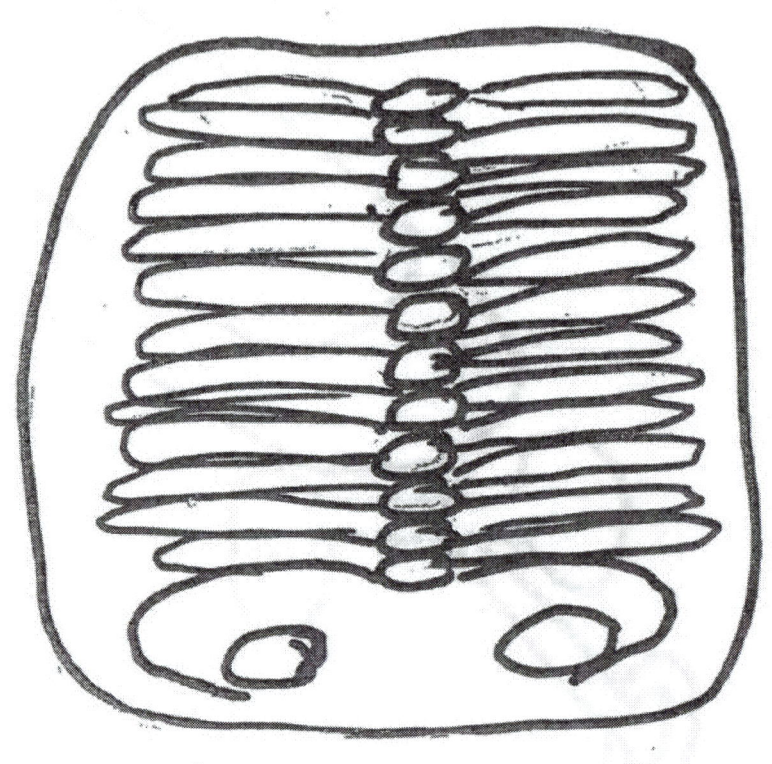

24. x...x...x-ray

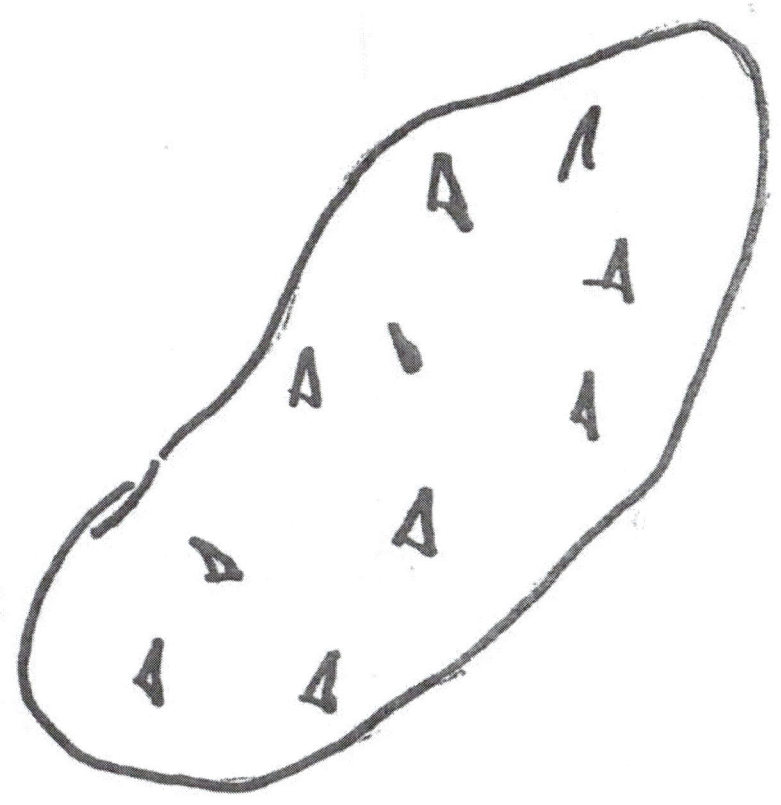

25. y...y...yam

26. z...z...zebra

a b c d e

f g h i j k

l m n o p

q r s t u

v w x y z

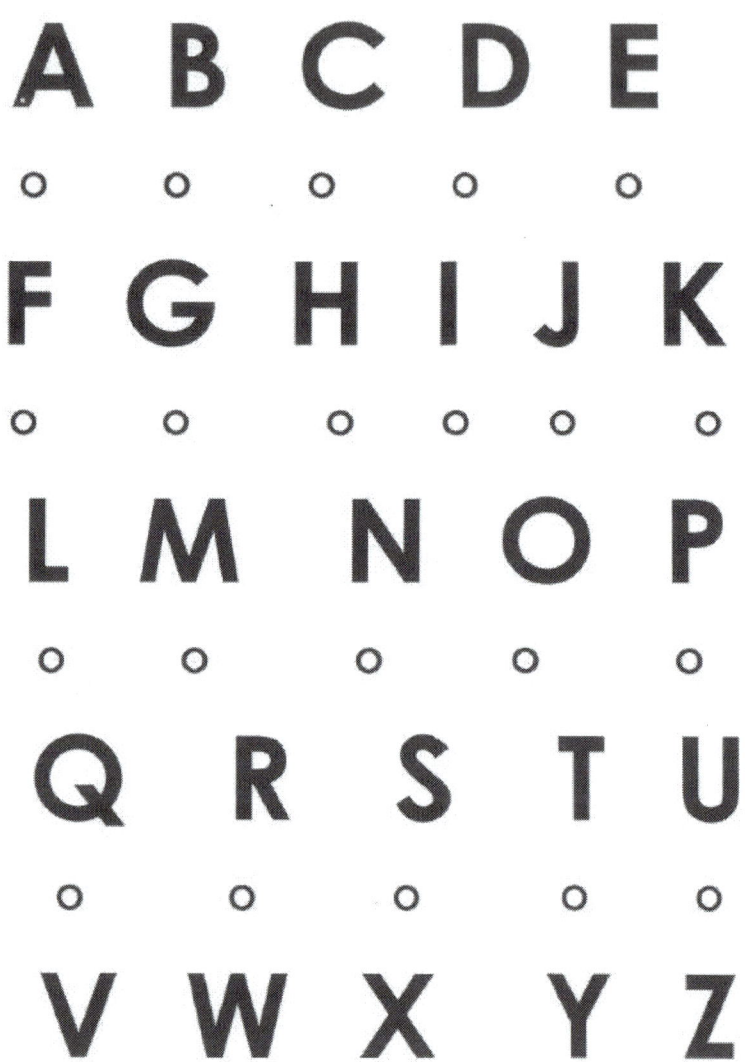

<u>at</u>

Book 1

Name _____

Read in 24 Lessons Birthright Linda Wilson @2019

1. a t   c at   cat

O O O O   O

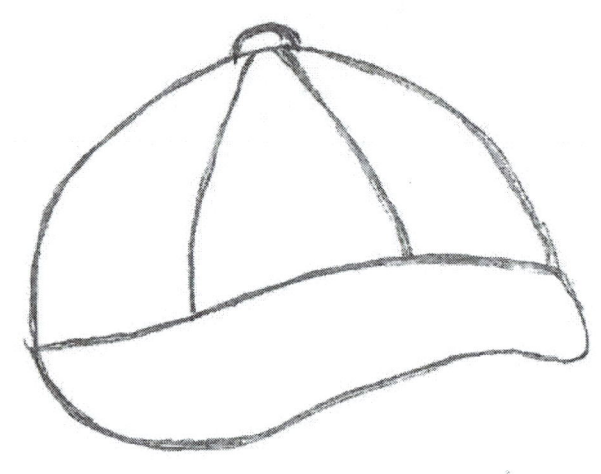

2. a t   h at   hat
   ○○   ○○   ○

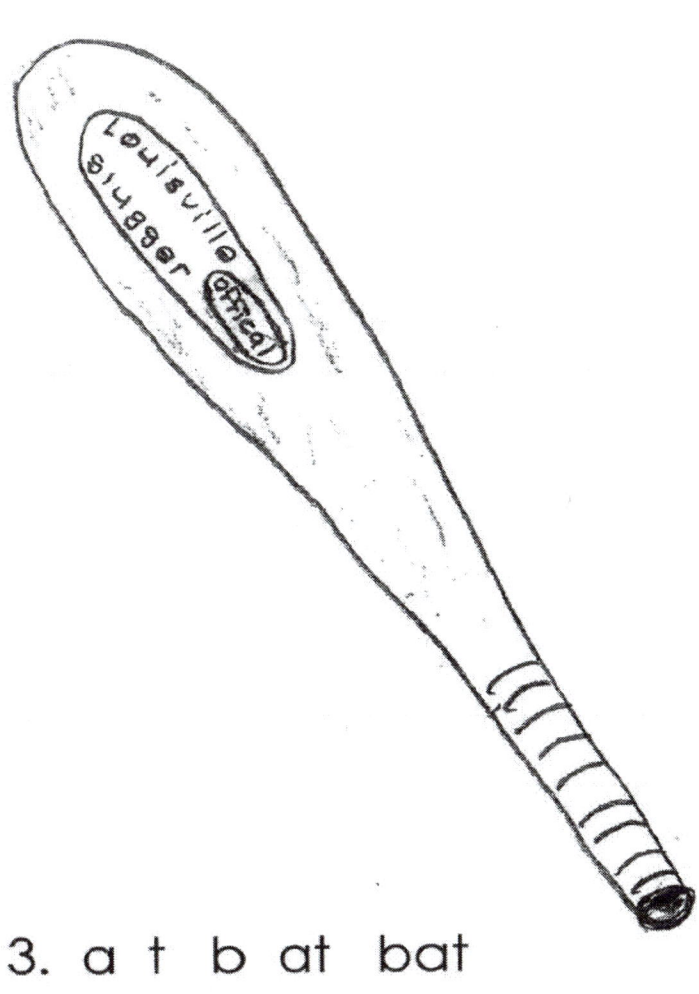

3. a t b at bat

○ ○ ○ ○ ○

4. a t m at mat

○ ○ ○ ○ ○

5. a t P at Pat

◯ ◯ ◯ ◯ ◯

6. a t   s at   sat

◯◯   ◯◯   ◯

sound	read
a t	at
O O	O
Sound	read
a t	at
O O	O

ran

Book 2

Name_____

Read in 24 Lessons Birthright ℗ 2019 Linda Wilson 𝓛𝔀

1 A nn   Ann

O O   O

2   r   a   n   ran

O   O   O   O

3 N a n   Nan ran!
O O O   O   O

4　r a t　rat　ran

O　OO　O　O

5   t a n   tan rat
  ○ ○ ○ · ○ ○

6 Tan rat ran.

O   O   O

7   Tan Ann ran.

O   O   O

8 Tan Nan ran.

O   O   O

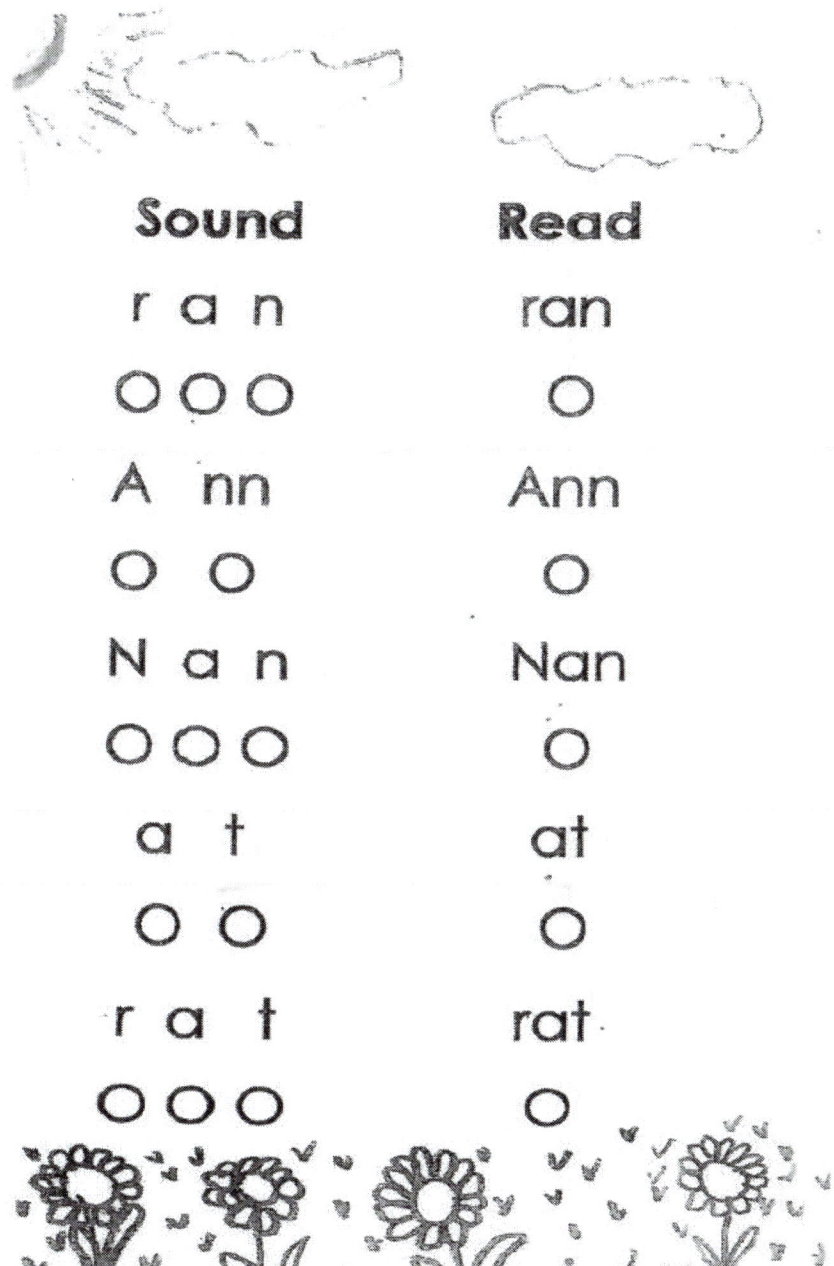

Sound	Read
r a n	ran
O O O	O
A nn	Ann
O O	O
N a n	Nan
O O O	O
a t	at
O O	O
r a t	rat
O O O	O

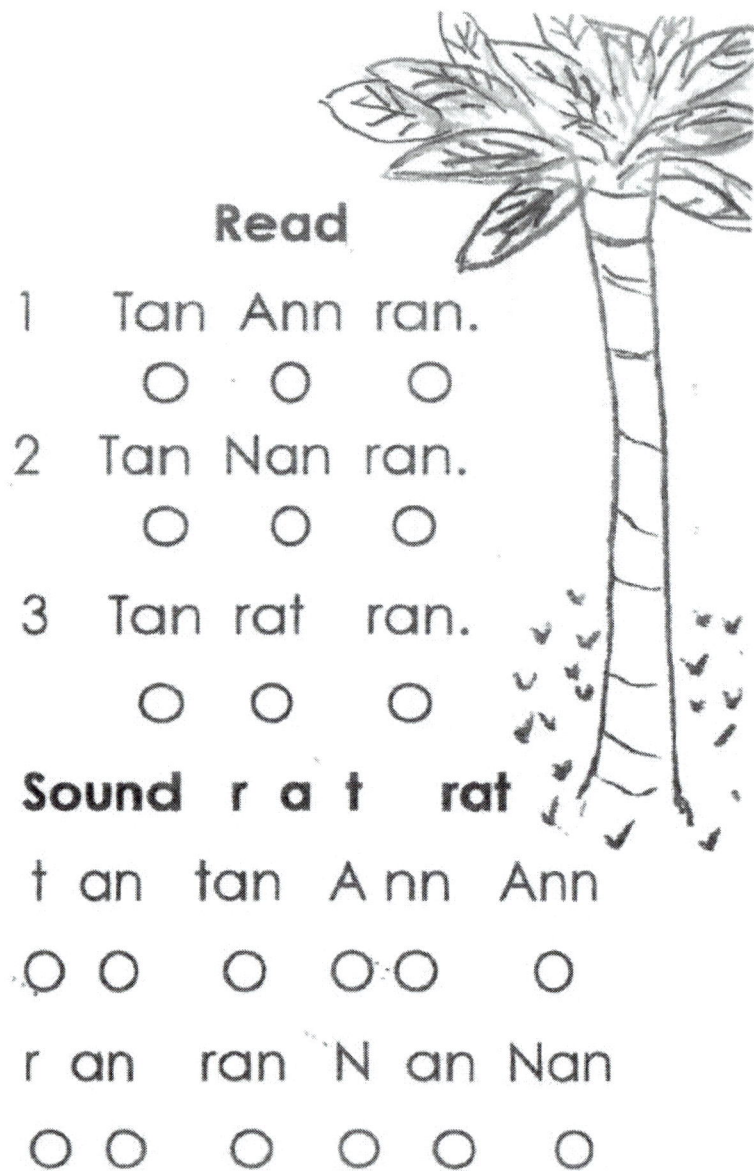

Read

1 Tan Ann ran.
   O   O   O

2 Tan Nan ran.
   O   O   O

3 Tan rat ran.
   O   O   O

Sound r a t   rat

t an tan A nn Ann
O O   O   O O   O

r an ran N an Nan
O O   O   O O   O

N N ___ ___ ___

n n ___ ___ ___

R R ___ ___ ___

r r ___ ___ ___

I to

a A

Book 3

Name_____

Read in 24 Lessons Birthright ©2019 Linda Wilson *LW.*

to

moo

boo

1 t o to t o to
o o o o o o

2 I ran to Rat.

O O O O

3 Ann ran to Rat.

O   O O   O

4 Nan ran to Rat.

O   O O   O

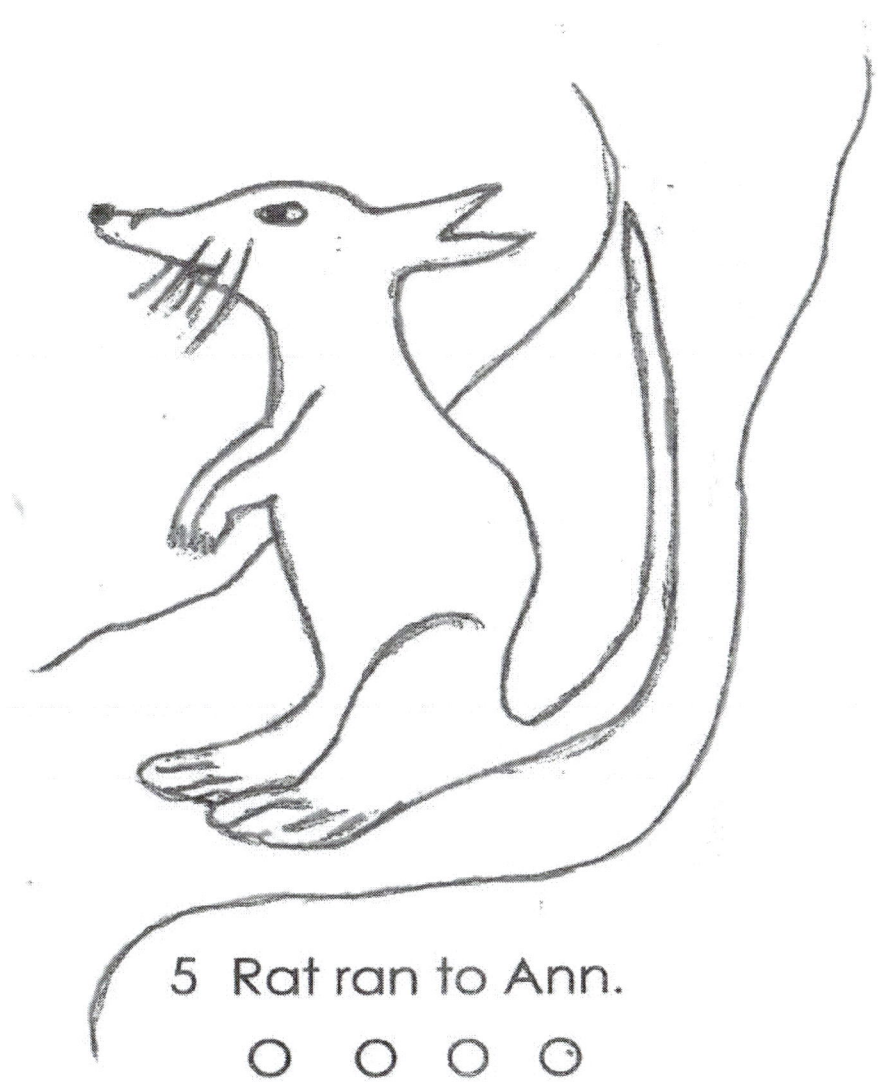

5 Rat ran to Ann.

○ ○ ○ ○

6 I ran to Ann.

O   O   O   O

7 Nan ran to Ann.

O   O O   O

8 I ran to Nan.

O O O O

9 Ann ran to Nan.

O   O O   O

10 Rat ran to Nan.

O O O O

I __ __

to __

a __ A __

A rat ran!
O O   O

I ran to a rat.
O O O O O

Cc the

go can

Book 4

Name _____

Read in 24 Lessons Birthright ⓒ 2019 Linda L. Wilson ℒ𝓌

Sound **Read**

1 c a t   c a n   cat can

O O O   O O O   O   O

2 g o go Cat can go.
○ ○ ○   ○   ○ ○

3 The   The cat can go.

O   O   O   O   O

5 Nan can go.

6 I can go to the cat.

○ ○ ○ ○ ○ ○

7 The cat can go to Ann.

○   ○   ○   ○   ○   ○

8. The cat can go to Nan.

O O O O O O

9 Can cat go? Cat can go, go, go.

O O O O O O O O

Make a Word Wall

I	an	at	aA
a	can	cat	tT
A	ran	rat	rR
to	Nan		nN
the	Ann		cC
go	tan		

Make 2 Vowel Hands

Say Short Sounds-Say Long Sounds

C____ c____

go_____

th_____

the quiet e

sound read

c a t cat

c a n can

<u>Mm</u> <u>Dd</u> <u>am</u>

<u>and</u> <u>too</u>

Book 5

Name_____

Read in 24 Lessons Birthright © 2019 Linda Wilso

<u>Words</u> <u>and</u> <u>Sounds</u> <u>Wall</u>

Mm	<u>am</u>	<u>an</u>	<u>at</u>
Dd	Cam	man	Matt
Cc	ram	Dan	mat
Rr	Tam	can	cat
Nn	<u>ad</u>	ran	rat
Tt	Tad	tan	<u>**to**</u>
Aa	add	Nan	too
I	dad	Ann	who
Aa	mad	**the, and, go**	

1. Dan and Matt can add.

O   O   O   O   O

Who can add?

1. Dan
2. Matt

2.   1 + 1 = 2

○ ○ ○ ○ ○

3. Tad ran to Ann. Ann

〇 〇 〇 〇   〇

and Tad can add.

〇 〇 〇 〇

Who can add?

1. Dan

2. Matt

3. Tad

4. Ann

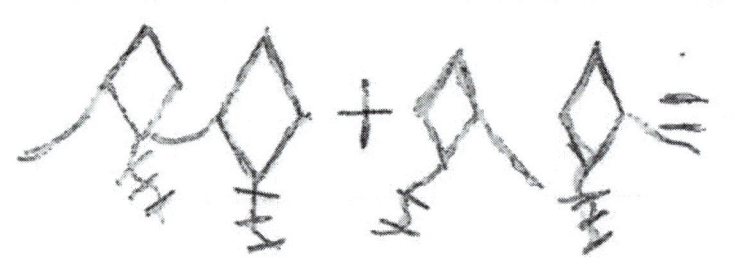

4.   2 + 2 = 4

O O O O O

5. Nan and Cam can add too.

○   ○   ○   ○   ○   ○

Who can add?

1. Dan	6. Cam
2. Matt	
3. Tad	
4. Ann	
5. Nan	

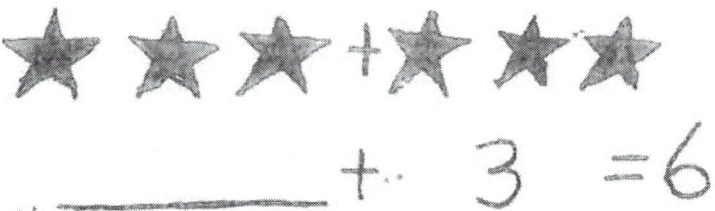

$$\underline{\qquad} + 3 = 6$$

6.   3 + 3 = 6

○ ○ ○○○

7. I am Tam. I can add.

○ ○ ○ ○ ○ ○

Who can add?

1. Dan	6. Cam
2. Matt	7. Tam
3. Tad	8. Dad
4. Ann	
5. Nan	

8. Dad can add too. 4 + 4 = 8

9. Can the man and the

○ ○ ○ ○ ○

mad ram at the mat add?

○ ○ ○ ○ ○ ○

Who can add?

1. Dan	6. Cam
2. Matt	7. Tam
3. Tad	8. Dad
4. Ann	9. A Man
5. Nan	10. A Ram

10 can add!

5 + 5=10   11111+11111

10. The man and the ram can add.

○   ○   ○   ○   ○   ○

M _____   _____   _____

m _____   _____   _____

D _____   _____   _____

d _____   _____   _____

Sound	Read	Sound	Read
a n d	and	t oo	too
O O O	O	O O	O
a m	am	w h o	who
O O	O	quiet w O O	O

Pp Ss so who no
Book 6

Name _____

Read in 24 Lessons © 2019 L. Wilson *Lw*

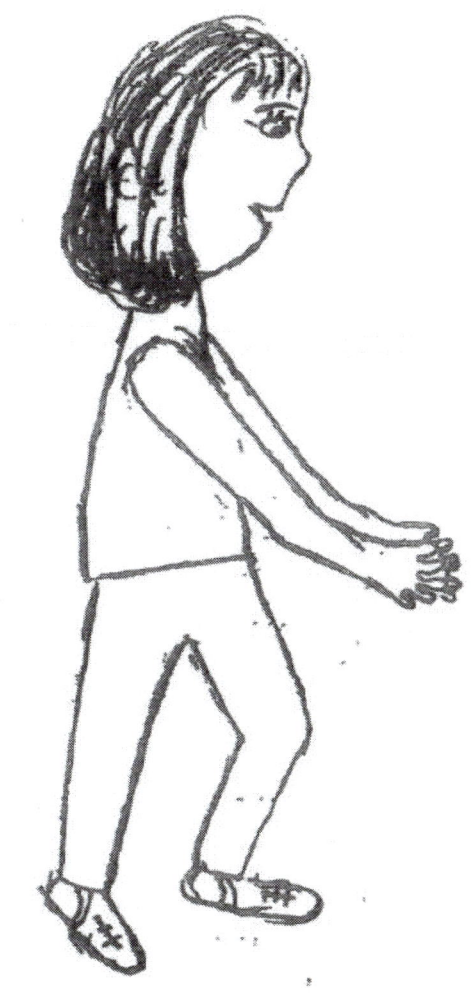

1   Go, Pat, go! Pat ran and ran.

O   O   O   O   O   O   O

2 Go, Sam go! Sam ran and ran.

O   O   O   O   O   O   O

3 Go Pam go! Pam ran and ran.

O O O   O O O O

4 Pat, Sam and Pam ran

O   O   O   O   O

and ran to the tan sand.

O   O   O   O   O   O

5 Who **is** at the tan sand ?

O O O O O O

6 Sad cat **is** at the tan sand.

O O OO O O O

I am at the tan sand too.

O O O O O O O

7 Sad cat **is** at a tan sand mat.

O   O O O O O   O   O

8 Can sad cat go? No! I pat

O O O O   O O O

and pat, the sad, sad, cat.

O   O   O   O   O   O

9   So, can sad cat go?

○   ○   ○   ○   ○

Sad cat **can** go, and I can go.

○   ○   ○   ○ ○ ○   ○   ○

Pat, Sam and Pam can go too!

○   ○   ○   ○   ○   ○   ○

Book 6

Make a Word Wall

Say the name!   Say the sound!

Pp Ss Mm Dd Cc Rr Nn Tt Aa I Aa

Word Wall – New Words – **Bold**

and	am	an	ad	at	ap
sand	**Sam**	**pan**	sad	**sat**	sap
	Pam	tan	**pad**	**pat**	cap
as	ram	Dan	add	mat	**map**
	Tam	can	mad	Matt	**tap**
go	Cam	Nan	dad	cat	**nap**
no		Ann	Tad	rat	
so	the			to	
		is (short i Bk 7)		too	
			(quiet w)	**who**	

132

P ___ ___ ___

p ___ ___ ___

S ___ ___ ___

S ___ ___ ___

Sound	Read	Sound	Read
P a m	Pam	n o	no
o o o	o	o o	o
s a n d	sand	s o	so

Ii it in is did
into do
Book 7

Name _____

Read in 24 Lessons© 2018 Birthright Linda Wilson

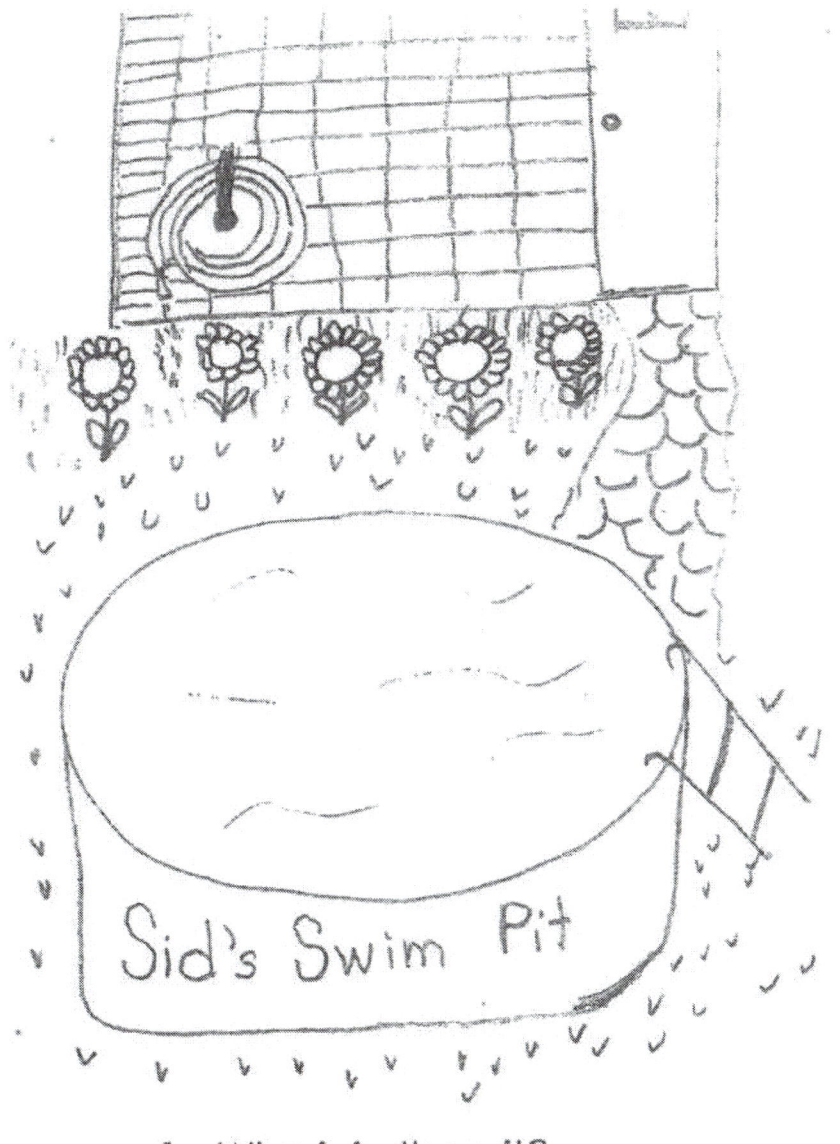

Sid's Swim Pit

1 Who is in the pit?

O OO O O

✓ 2   Sid is in the pit.

○ ○ ○ ○ ○

3 Sid can sit in it.

○ ○ ○○○

4   Did Miss Sis go in the pit?

O   O   O   O   O   O   O

Sid's Swim Pit

5 Miss Sis can do it. Miss Sis

O O O .O OO O O

can sit and dip in the pit.

O O O O OO O O

6   Who is this?   It is Pip.

○ ○ ○   ○ ○ ○

7 Pip can rip, nip and tip.

O O O O O O

8 Pip ran into the pit.

O   O   O   O   O

Sid's Swim Pit

9 Sid, Sis and Pip sit in

O O O O O O

the pit and sip, sip, sip.

O O O O O O

Say the name! Say the sound!

Ii Pp Ss Mm Dd Cc Rr Nn Tt Aa I Aa

Word Wall			sound	sound
is	ip	id	d i d	m i ss
Sis	sip	Sid	O O O	O O O
Miss	dip	did	s i p	p i t
it	rip	rid	O O O	O O O
sit	nip	the	s i t	r i p
pit	Pip	this	O O O	O O O
mitt	tip	that	i n t o	S i d
in	to	go	O O OO	O O O
sin	too	no	i s	th i s
pin	who	so	O O	O O O
tin	do		p i n	r i d
	into		O O O	O O O

I _____ _____ _____ _____ _____

i _____ _____ _____ _____ _____

is _____ _____ _____

in_____ _____ _____

it _____ _____ _____

do _____ _____ _____

did _____ _____

into _____

Hh have

my

Book 8

Name _____

Read in 24 Lessons Birthright ⊜2019 L. Wilson

1. **Hap has his mitt.**

○ ○ ○ ○

2 **I have my hat.**

○   ○   ○   ○

3 **Sid has his cap in his hand.**

○   ○ ○   ○ ○ ○   ○

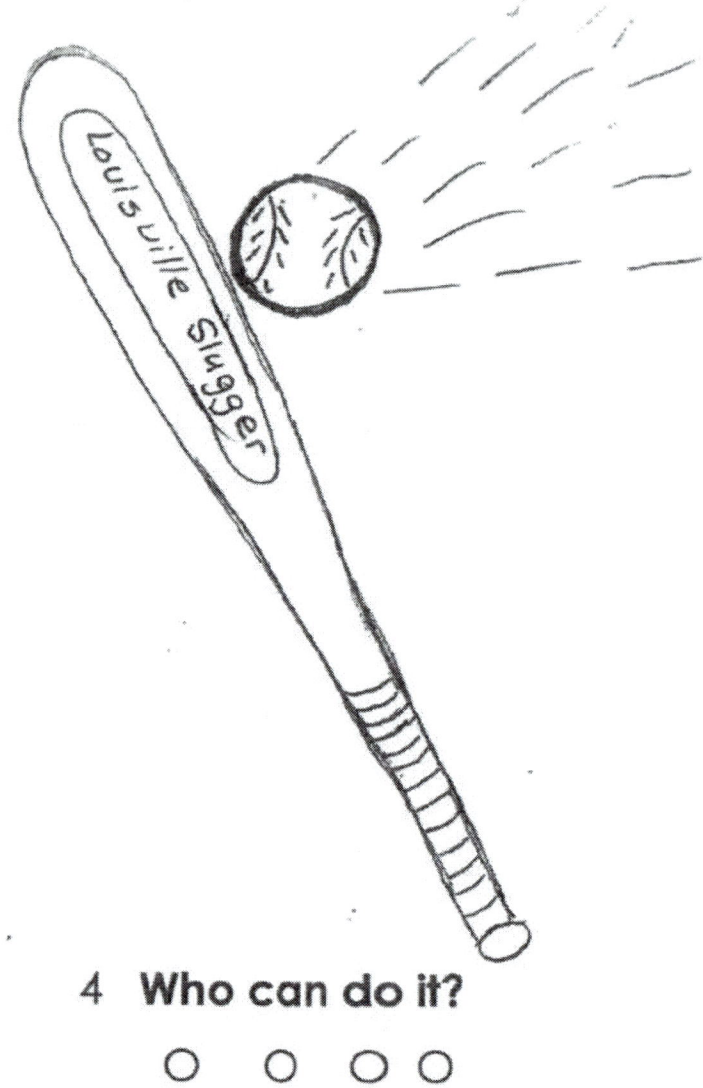

4 **Who can do it?**

○   ○   ○ ○

Cats

5   **Sam can!**

○   ○

6 **Sam can tip his hip.**

○   ○ ○ ○ ○

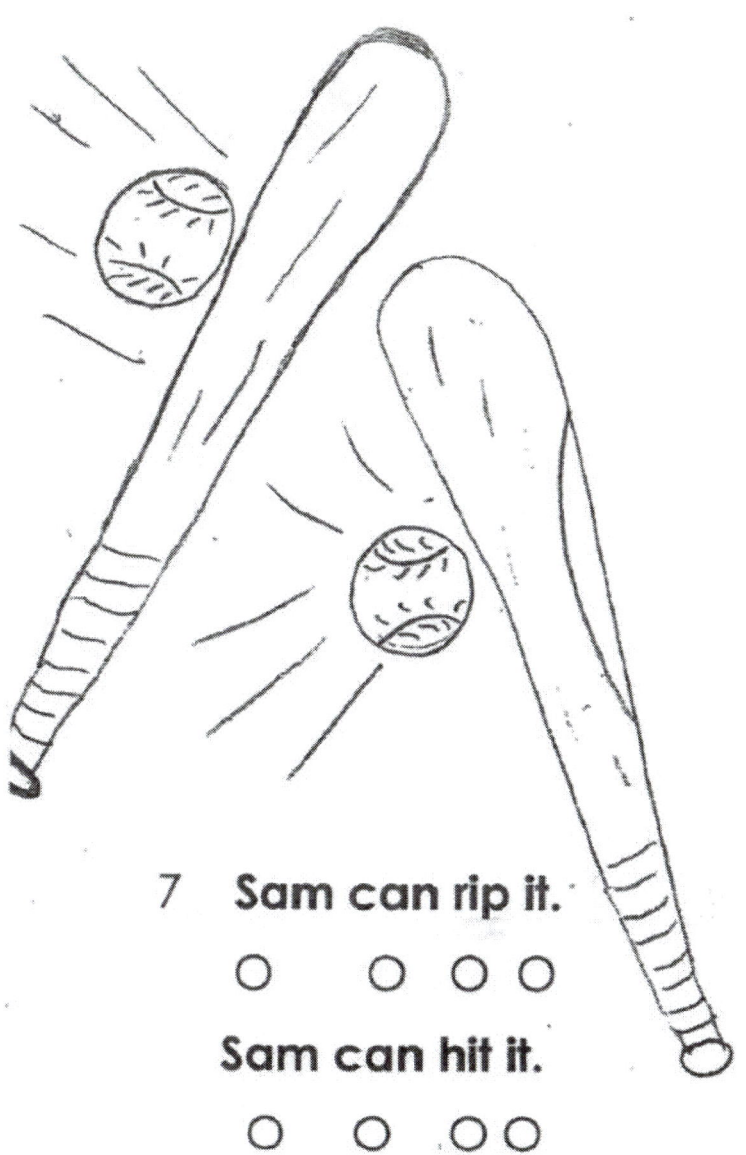

7 **Sam can rip it.**

    O   O O O

Sam can hit it.

    O   O .O O

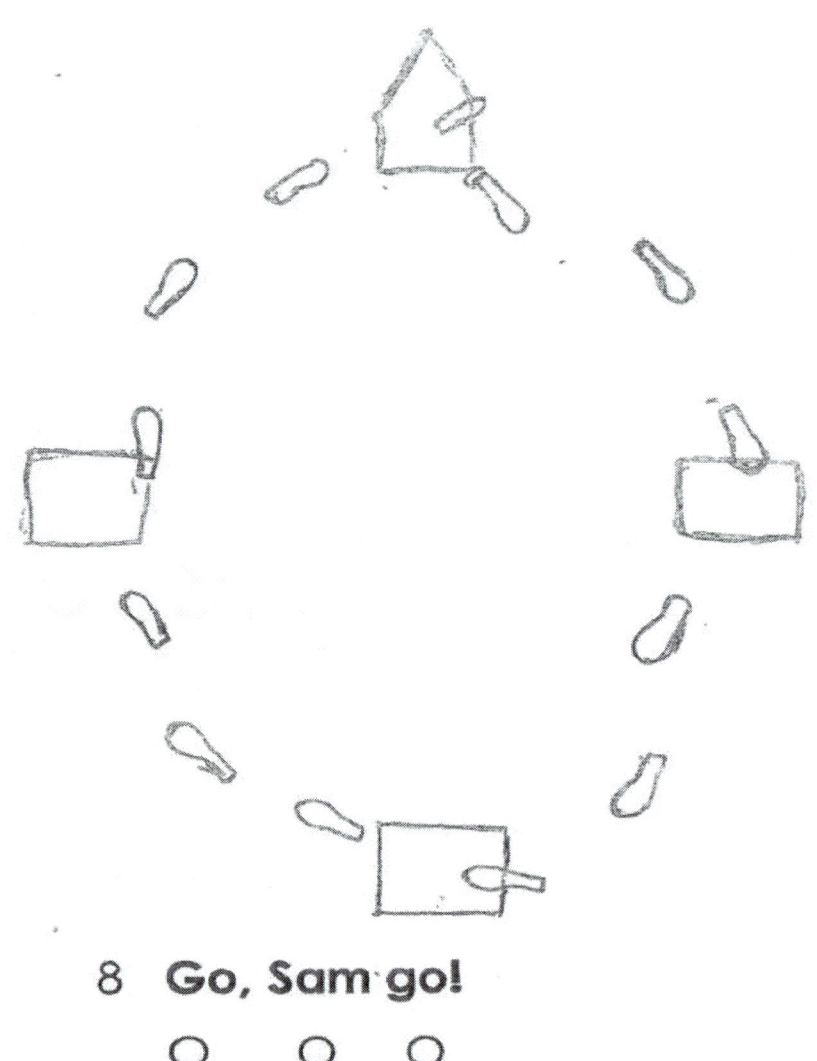

8 **Go, Sam go!**

O   O   O

9 **Ho, Ho, Ho! Go, Go, Go!**

○ ○ ○ ○ ○ ○

Sound - <u>Hh</u> Ii Pp Ss Mm
Dd Cc Rr Nn Tt Aa I Aa
<u>Word Wall</u> – Sound & Read

and	**am**	**ad**	**at**
hand	ham	had	hat
is	**ip**	**id**	**it**
his	hip	hid	hit
iss	**go**	**my** (y says i)	
hiss	Ho Ho	cry	

have (short a quiet e)

give, live (short i quiet e)

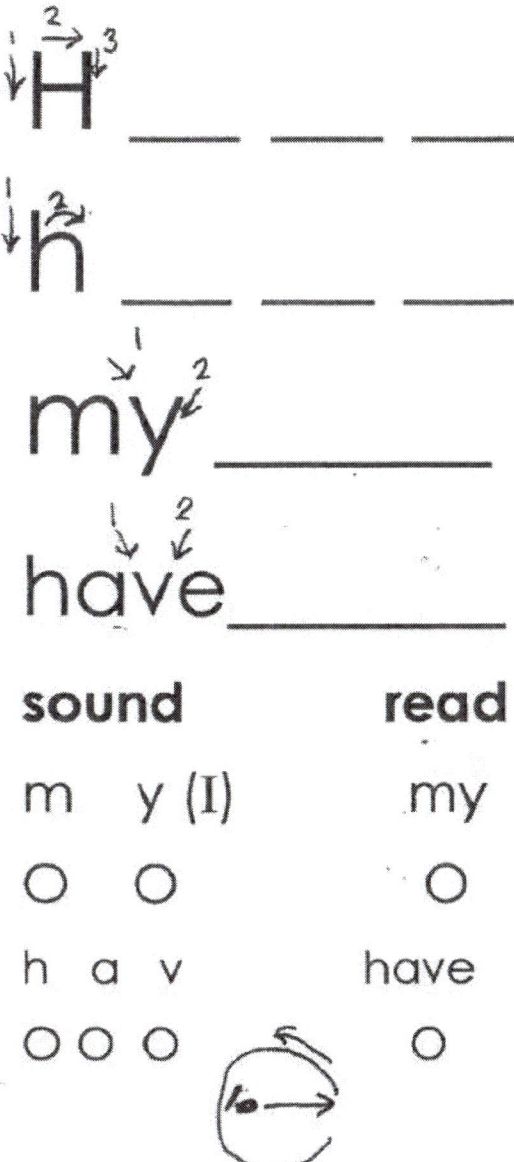

H _____ _____ _____

h _____ _____ _____

my _____

have _____

sound   **read**

m   y (I)   my

O   O   O

h   a   v   have

O O O   O

Bb Gg big
this that

Book 9

Name_____

Read in 24 Lessons <u>Birthright</u> ℗ 2019 Wilson *Ƚⱳ*

1 Who did it? Who hid Dad's ham?

O   OO   O   O   O   O

2 Pig has ham in his hand.

○ ○ ○   ○ ○   ○

3 This is Big Pig's ham.

○ ○ ○ ○ ○

That is Dad's missing ham.

○ ○ ○ ○ ○

4 **Big Pig is singing and going**

○ ○○ ○ ○ ○

to his big rig. No ham!

○ ○ ○ ○ ○ ○

5 The band is going to a cab.

○   ○   ○   ○   ○ ○ ○

The singing band has ham.

○   ○   ○   ○   ○

6 **Did the band nab the ham?**

○   ○   ○   ○   ○   ○

Dad's napping.   Go, Dad, go!

○   ○   ○   ○   ○

7 **Is Dad mad? No! Is Dad**

○   ○   ○   ○   ○ ○

sad? No! The band can go.

○   ○   ○   ○   ○ ○

8 Dad has his missing ham.

○　○　○　　○　　　○

So, this is my ham too.

○　○ ○○　　○　　○

Dad and I have the ham!

○　　○ ○ ○　　○　　○

Dad's Ham-Yum!

Sound/Read

ing   D a d   the

O   O O O   O

s ing   Dad   th at

O O   O   O   O

sing   Dad's   that

O   O   O

singing miss   th is

O   O   O   O

go ing missing   this

O   O   O   O

going   nap napping

Book 9 Word Wall Sound/Read

Bb **Gg** Hh Ii Pp Ss Mm

Dd Cc Rr Nn Tt Aa I Aa

ib   ig   ag   ap   ab

bib   big   bag   gap   gab

rib   dig   rag   map   nab

     pig   sag   nap   tab

it   rig   tag   cap   cab

bit (the, this, that) (have, give)

at   ing   ang   and   my

bat   sing   sang   band   by

id   ring   rang

bid   going   (Dad, Dad's)

     missing

     napping singing ringing

B _____ _____ _____

b _____ _____ _____

G _____ _____ _____

g _____ _____ _____

Read Bb

big   bag

nab   bad

bit   bib

gab   cab

nab   band

Read Gg

bag   gab

big   sang

dig   sing

tag   rag

pig   rig

L l Kk ck

little black

all

Book 10

Name _____

Birthright ℗2019

Read in 24 Lessons Linda Wilson ℒ𝓌

1 King Rick has a little black

○ ○ ○ ○○ ○

cat who is sick.

○ ○ ○ ○

2 **All little Lil can do is meow!**

O O O O O O O

3 **King Rick bit his lip.**

O   O   O O   O

He can call Dr. Bill.

O   O   O   O   O

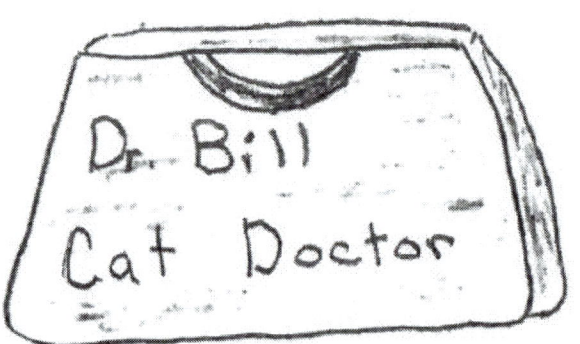

4 **Dr. Bill has a cat pill.**

O O O O O O

It is in his black kit.

O O O O   O   O

5 **Dr. Bill is a pal. Lil ran to**

○ ○○○○ ○ ○ ○

him and did a lick kiss.

○ ○ ○○○ ○

6 **King Rick has Lil in his**

O   O   O O O O

hand. Little Lil is back!

O   O O O   O

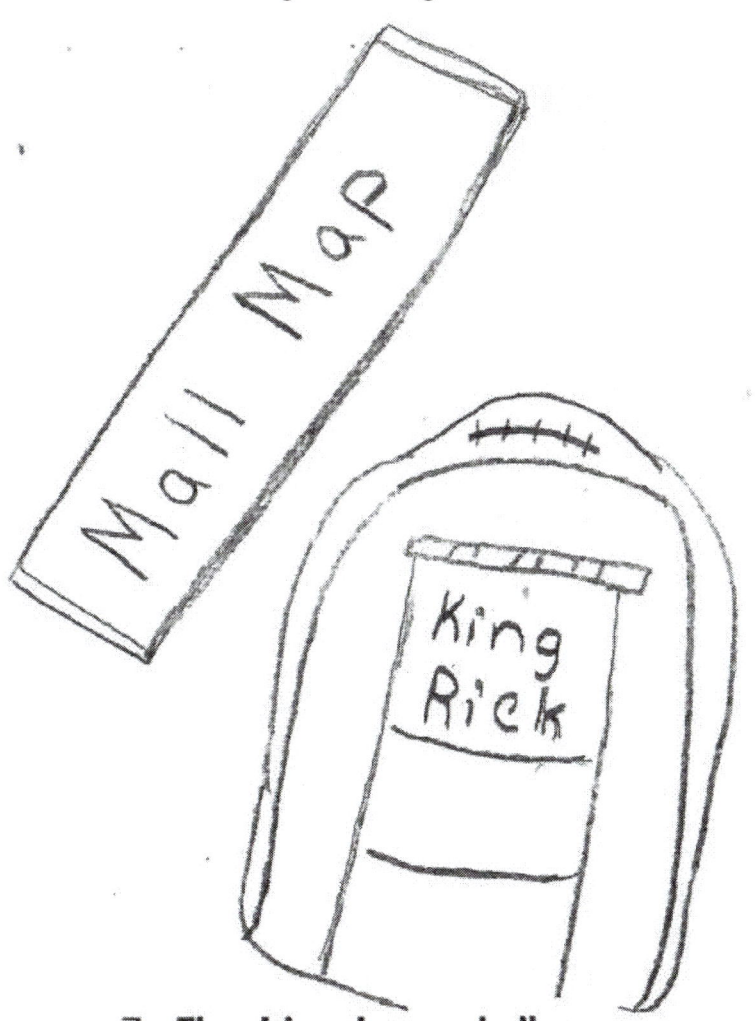

7 **The king has a tall map**

○ ○ ○ ○ ○ ○

and a backpack.

○ ○   ○

8 He and Lil can go to the

○ ○ ○ ○ ○ ○ ○

mall and have a ball.

○ ○ ○ ○ ○

Book 10 Word Wall

Ll Kk ck Bb Gg Hh Ii Pp Ss

Mm Dd Cc Rr Nn Tt Aa I Aa

Al	ack	ick	ill	id
pal	**black**	lick	Lil	lid
Sal	back	kick	pill	kid
all	pack	pick	till	ap
ball	sack	Rick	hill	lap
tall	rack	Dick	iss	ab
call	Mack	Nick	kiss	lab
mall	lack	tick	ip	ad
and	it kit	ing	lip	lad
land	lit **little**	king	Kip	

We know these **Dolch Words**!

black little all this

that big have my

it in is did into do

so who no and

am too the go I

can a to A ran at

In this lesson, we introduced

Me-ow! It has 2 new sounds.

m<u>e</u>-s<u>ee</u>, h<u>e</u>, w<u>e</u>, thr<u>ee</u>-long <u>e</u>

<u>ow</u>- d<u>ow</u>n, <u>ou</u>t, n<u>ow</u>, br<u>ow</u>n

We can read over 200 words.

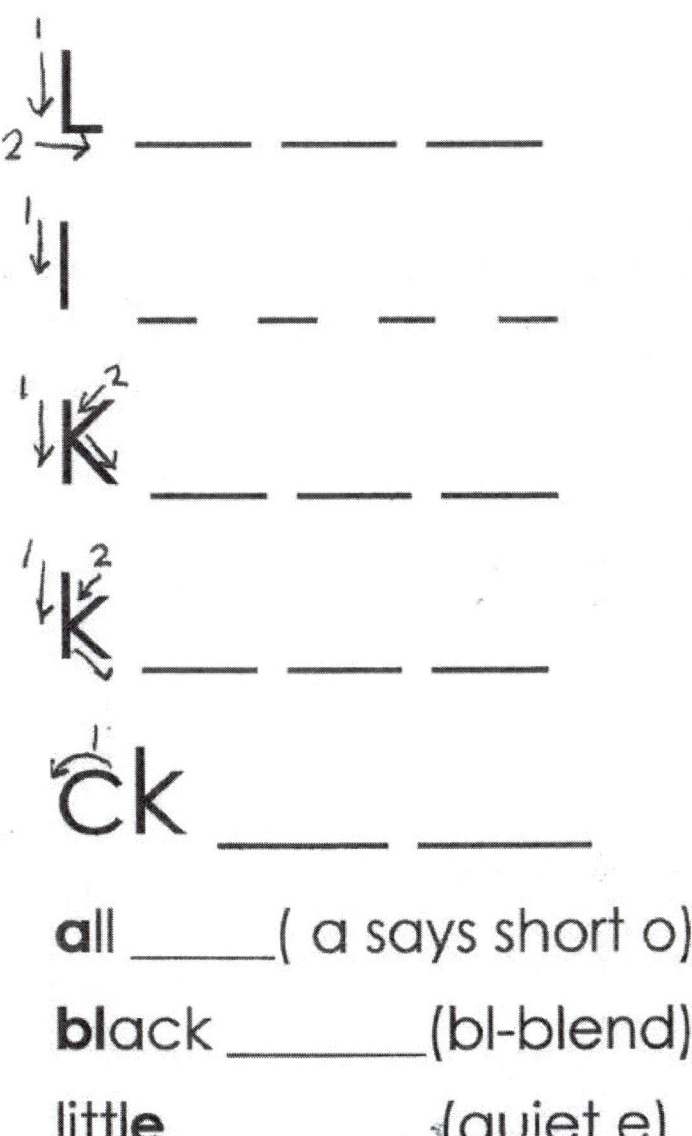

all _____(a says short o)

black _____(bl-blend)

little _____(quiet e)

Jj Uu jump up but run must come

Book 11

Name _____

Read in 24 Lessons @ 2019 Birthright Linda Wilson ℱ𝓌

1 Jo Jo is just a cat. But, Jo Jo can run, jump and fly.

2 **The sun is up. Jo Jo must fly to Little Kim and Big Jim.**

3 **Jip, a bad mutt, is digging up the dump.**

4 **Jo Jo must fly to the dump.**

5 **Jip has a little pup. His**

pup is sick. Bad mutt is

just a sad dad.

6 **Jo Jo calls Kim and Jim**

to come to the dump.

7 **The kids come and give**

sick little pup a big hug.

8 " By little Pup. By Jip." Kim

and Jim pack up and go.

" By Kim, Jim and Jo Jo." The

pups pick up and go.

But, can Jo Jo the cat just

go? No! Jo Jo must run,

jump and fly in the sky!

Book 11 Dolch & Word Wall

Dolch Words To Date

up run but must jump <u>come</u>

come (o says short u)(some)

black little all this that big

have my it in is did into do

so who no and am too the

go I can a to A ran at

Letters & Sounds To Date

Jj Uu Bb Gg Hh Ii Pp Ss Mm

Dd Cc Rr Nn Tt Aa I Aa

Sounds – th oo o v   **sky**

my (y says i) **fly** dry try cry **by**

up	**ump**	**ust**	**ut**	**un**
pup	**jump**	**must**	**but**	**run**
cup	dump	dust	cut	bun
ub	hump	rust	hut	sun
rub	bump	bust	mutt	hum
tub	pump	crust	rut	**uck**
sub	**ug**	**us**	nut	duck
hub	bug	bus	**ud**	buck
um	hug	Gus	bud	truck
gum	tug	**am**	dud	luck
an	rug	jam	**im**	tuck
Jan	lug	**ack**	Jim	**ill**
ab - jab	Jack	**go**-Jo	Jill

J _____ _____ _____

j _____ _____ _____

U _____ _____ _____

U _____ _____ _____

jump _____

but _____ _____

up _____ _____

run _____ _____

must _____

come (o says short u) _____

Yy Vv

want say

they yes

Book 12

Name _____

Read in 24 Lessons ©2019 Birthright Wilson

1 My, it is a sunny day. Vic, Val

and Viv want to go to the beach.

2 Say, can Dad go too? Yes,
Dad wants to go in the van.

3   **They all go to the beach**

in the big van.

4 **At the beach, they jump and run in the tan sand.**

5 **A big wave comes by, and they jump into it. A little wave comes by, and they run to it.**

6 **Vic, Viv, Val and Dad go to**

The Beach Hut. At The Beach

Hut, they run into Gus and Al.

7 **Yum, Dad and the kids have ham on a big bun. And, they all buy a tan yo-yo.**

8 "Yes," they all say. "This is the
day to have fun at the beach."

<u>Word Wall - New Dolch **Bold**</u>

say want they yes <u>have</u> (<u>review</u>)

yes (short vowel **e**-consonant **y**)

up run but must jump come all

black little this that big my it is

have in did into do who no am

too and the go I can a to A ran

so at **Vv Yy** <u>Jj Uu Bb Gg Hh Ii Pp</u>

<u>Ss Dd Kk Ll Mm Cc Rr Nn Tt Aa I</u>

Short Vowel Sounds-Uu Aa Ii Ee

Long Vowel Sounds-Aa Oo Ii Ee

Sounds–th(the) o(to) ch(beach)

am-**yam**, ic-**Vic**, al-**Val**, ip-**yip**

go-**yo-yo**, av-**have**, an-**van**

iv- **live give Viv** um-**yum** es-**yes**

Sound

s u n   sun   s u nn y   sunny

OOO   O   OO OO   O

s ay   say   d ay   day

O O   O   O O   O

w **a** nt w**a**nt y e s yes

O O O   O   OOO O

<u>w**a**</u>nt(**a**-short u) <u>w**a**ve</u>(lg a)

<u>be**a**ch</u>(long e&digraph ch)

<u>s**ay**</u> (long a) <u>they</u> (long a)

<u>m**y**</u> (y- long i) <u>ye**s**</u> (consonant)

<u>sunn**y**</u> (y says long e)

Y _____ _____ _____

y _____ _____ _____ _____

V _____ _____ _____

v _____ _____ _____

want _____

say _____

they _____

yes _____

have _____

Ee Ff

help said

funny red

pretty get

Book 13

Name _____

Read in 24 Lessons ℗2019 Birthright Linda L. Wilson

1   Ed said, " This is
pretty funny."

A bed fit for a king Duck - Ned

2 "Jed and Ted get a red
bed for Ned the duck."

3 Nell said, " I can yell, yell, yell."

4 "I want to sell, sell,

sell my big, big bell."

5 Jen said, "I can help
my best pal Ben."

6 "Ben and I want to make a pen for his little red hen."

7 Bev said, "This is the best test."

Bev's Spelling Test

1 fan	2 fun
3 fig	4 fell
5 fib	6 fit
7 fat	8 fast
9 fed	10 fin

Sentence

A funny duck fell in the mud.

8 "That is pretty Miss Peg who helps us spell."

Word Wall   Book 13

Aa Bb Cc Dd **Ee Ff**

Gg Hh Ii Jj Kk Ll Mm

Nn Pp Rr Ss Tt Uu Vv

Yy **eb**　**et**　**Ed**　**egg**

key Jeb bet bed Peg

en Deb jet **red** Meg

hen **ell** **get** **said** leg

pen bell met fed beg

Ben sell net led **elp**

Jen tell set Ned **help**

ten fell **pretty** Jed yelp

Dolch Words

get help pretty said red
funny at I a A to ran
the go can am and so
too who no it in is did
into do have my big all
this that little black jump
they but run must come
up want say they yes
s**ai**d (ai says short e)
f**u**nn**y**(u short / y long e)
pr**e**tty(pr blend/short e/y long e)

E _____ _____

e _____ _____

F _____ _____

f _____ _____

get _____

help _____

pretty _____

said _____

funny _____

Ww will well went what one with was where

Book 14

Introduction to AR

Name_____

Read in 24 Lessons ©2019 Birthright Linda Wilson *Lw*

1 Wes and Will went to
sleep in the tent.

2 The next day they said,

"What can we do?"

3 Wes said, " We can
go to the wishing well."

4 "That was fun when
we went with Kent."

5 Will said, "Off we go!"

6 " This will be one fun
day!"

Parents and Teachers,

It is time to introduce our new readers to AR, accelerated reading. AR books are library books with reading levels. After reading the AR book, the student takes a five question computer test.

Students earn reading points for every successful score of 80 to100%. Most schools offer prizes or rewards with AR points earned. The books we will be reading are worth ½ a point. So, 20 books could earn 10 points.

To date, we know 52 Dolch words. There are 40 words left to learn. We also know 30 of our 43 sounds. Yes, it is time for early library books.

I suggest you start with <u>Oh, Cats!</u> by Nola Buck . Here's how to sound the new words. They are all Dolch words.

wh ae er = <u>where</u> (e- long a/er-r vowel)

pl ay – <u>play</u> (long a)   s ee – <u>see</u> (long e)

t o-<u>two</u> (quiet w)   thr ee– <u>three</u> (thr-blend)

ar e – <u>are</u> (ar/r vowel)   f i n d -<u>find</u> (lg i)

y oo – <u>you</u> (oo or lg u) d ow n-<u>down</u>)owl)

n ow- <u>now</u> (<u>owl</u>)   n o t – <u>not</u> (short o)

n ew –<u>new</u> (oo or lg u) l i k e – <u>like</u> (long i)

<u>Oh, Cats!</u> is totally a Dolch young reader book. Here are the new words in review.

<u>where, play, see, two, three, are, find,</u>

<u>you, down, now, not, new, like</u>

Another AR book is <u>Biscuit's Big Friend</u>

by Alyssa Capucilli. New words are carry, here, fetch, drink, there, fence, ready could.

Word Wall Book 14

Aa Bb Cc Dd Ee Ff Gg
Hh Ii Jj Kk Ll Mm Nn Pp
Rr Ss Tt Uu Vv **Ww** Yy

web wed wag **with**
wall **will well** wet Wes
wing west wam wig
who what when where
why **went** wish we win
one –(wun) **was** (wuz)

<u>What</u> do the boys do?
<u>Where</u> did they sleep?

Dolch Words Book 14

well went will with was

one where what help at I

ran the go can am and

a to so too who no it in is

did into do have my big

all this that little black

jump they but run must

come up want say they

said funny red pretty get

where – long a & r vowel

what – a says short o

W___ W___

what _____

well _____

went _____

will _____

with _____

was_____

one _____

where _____

Oo on

not saw

Book 15

Name _____

Read in 24 lessons © 2019 Birthright Linda L. Wilson

Short Vowel o Names

Bob Tom Rod Todd

Don Jon Ron Ross

oy Names

Roy   Joy

oy Words

boy toy

or Words

1   for four

Short Vowel Oo Things

clock

dock

lock

rock

2

More Short Vowel oO Things

pot

cot

dot

doll

top

3 mop

Short Vowel oO Actions

I lob the ball.

I sob.

I jog.

I hop.

I toss the ball.

ou Actions

I shout.

4

234

Turn the light **on** or off.

I **saw** moss on a log at

the pond.

5 My Pop is a good cop.

I can **not** go out into the fog.

The hog eats all of the corn

on the cob.

6 I also toss a ball to my dog.

or Words

Do not pout. I got the door

7 at the store for your room.

More AR Reading

Here is another great easy AR book. Jack and Jill and Big Dog Bill by Martin Weston - A Phonics Reader.

Here's more Biscuit books.

Biscuit Meets the Class Pet

Biscuit Finds a Friend

Biscuit and the Baby

Biscuit Goes to School

Biscuit Takes a Walk

Biscuit Wants to Play   8

Dolch Words-Book 15 Oo

Aa Bb Cc Dd Ee Ff Gg

Hh Ii Jj Kk Ll Mm Nn **Oo**

Pp Rr Ss Tt Uu Vv Ww Yy

n**o**t **on** s**aw**(like short o)

will well went what one with

was where help at I ran the

go can am and to aA so too

who no it in is did into do my

have big all this that little but

black jump they run must up

come want say they said get

9   funny pretty said red

Word Wall

ob – Bob cob job lob

mob rob sob gob

ot – lot **not** pot rot tot

hot got dot jot cot

on – gone pong pond

oss - toss boss Ross moss

og -dog fog log jog hog

op - cop hop mop top

ck-clock dock rock lock

od – odd God Tod Rod

om – Tom mom pom

ŏ ___ o ___

not _____

on_____

saw_____

ou – out _____

ow – now _____

or – for ___ oi–oil ___

oy – boy _____

I want to say good-by!

☺

Consonant Digraphs

Book 16

ch sh wh th th

chin she why the

where what who

when they there

this that with

Name _____

In Book 1, what word has a **c**?

In Book 2, what name starts with the letter A?

There are 3 names in Book 3.
Write them.

_____

_____

_____

In Book 4, who can go, go, go?

2

Can the man and the mad ram add in Book 5?

Yes _____ No _____

In Book 6, Pat, Sam and Pam all ran. Where did they go?

_____ 3

In Book 7, who has a swim pit?

_____

Who gets in the pit with him?

_____

What does Hap have in Book 8?

_____

Who can hit the ball?

_____ 4

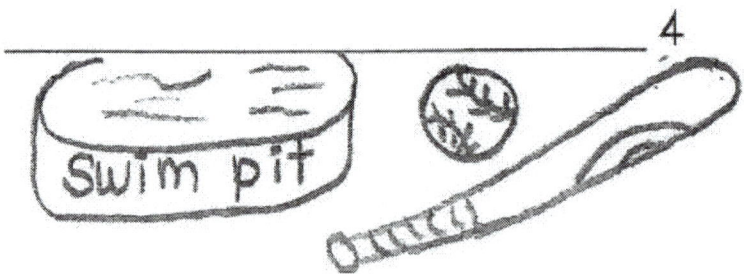

In Book 9, who has Dad's ham?

_____

Who gets in the big rig?

_____

Who is sick in Book 10?

_____

Where did Lil and King Rick go?

_____ 5

In Book 11, What can Jo Jo do?

_____

Who does Jo Jo help?

_____

In Book 12, who goes to the beach with Dad?

_____

What do they do when a big wave comes by?

_____ 6

In Book 13, who is Jen's pal?

_____

What can she do with him?

_____

In Book 14, what did Will and Wes do?

_____

In Book 15 what word rhymes with clock?

_____ 7

Have you read an AR book?

Yes _____ No_____

What book have you read?

Circle it!

Oh, Cats!

Jack and Jill and Big Dog Bill

Biscuit's Big Friend

Biscuit Wants to Play

Biscuit Goes to School

Biscuit Meets the Class Pet

Biscuit Finds a Friend

Biscuit Takes a Walk

Biscuit and the Baby   8

What book do you like best?

_____

Book 1   Book 2   Book 3

Book 4   Book 5   Book 6

Book 7   Book 8   Book 9

Book 10 Book 11   Book 12

Book 13 Book 14   Book 15

My AR Book

Book 8

Oh, Cats!

Write 3 sentences and tell why you like it.   9

_____

_____

_____

_____

_____

_____

_____

stop

chin_____

she _____

the _____

they_____

with _____

when _____

where_____

why _____

Read in 24 Lessons ⓔ2019 Wilson
Birthright LLC

R Vowels

are under

for four

Book 17

she there

where

Name _____

Read in 24 Lessons ℗2019 Birthright Wilson

1 I am Cory.

2 I am four.

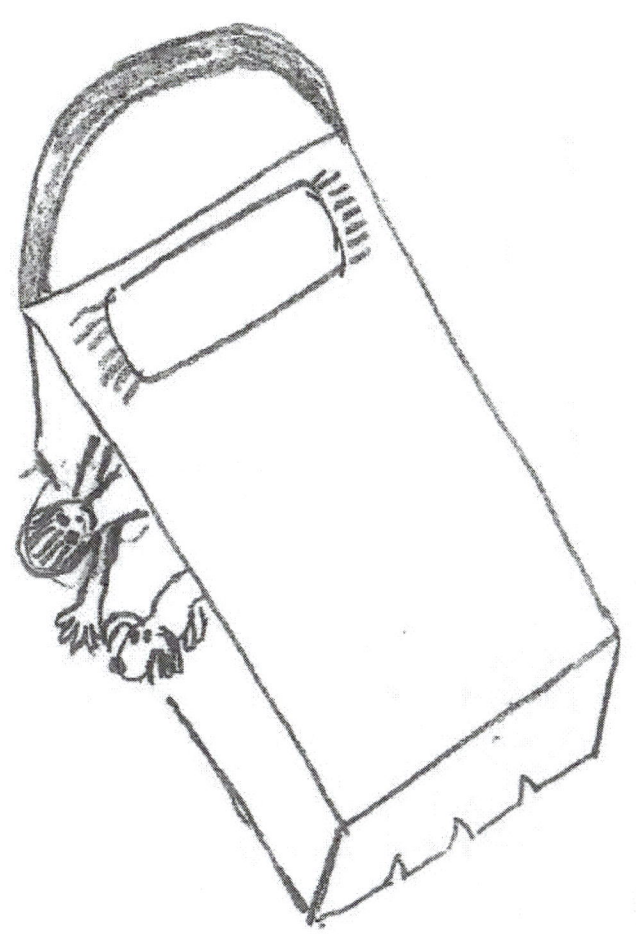

3 I go there. I go under
my bed with my dog Dory.

4 She and I play for the cats. Where do you play?

5 Are you four too?

R Vowels – Dolch - Book 17

ar- **are** car star jar far hard

er – **under** her sister ir- bird fir

or – **for four** more ur- burn

are under for four there she

not on saw will well went go

one with was where help at

what run the can am and to

all so who no it is in did into

do my have big all this that I

but little black jump they run

come want say they said up

pretty red must funny get   6

are _____

under _____

for _____

four _____

Review

she _____

there _____

where _____

Long Aa ate

make came

away play

Book 18

Review-say

they there

where

Name _____

Read in 24 Lessons ℗2019 Birthright Linda Wilson *Lw*

Dog and Cat Park
Dawn to Dusk
Sarasota County Parks

1 I came to play.

Do not run away!

2   Can we make up a game?

3 Say, they can play too.

4   Where can we play?

Can we play there?

5 We can have fun and play
in the sun. We can run, run, run.

Book 18 - Long Aa - Dolch

a_e   ay   e says a   a says u

ate   say   they   away

came away there about

make play where Linda

ate came make say play they what

away there where will yes with

a and big can come for funny

go help I jump little my not under

one red run said the up all on

am are at black but did do for

get have into must no pretty in

ran saw she so that this too is it

under want was well went to I

came_____

make_____

ate _____

play _____

away _____

say _____

they _____

there _____

Long Ee e - be

he me she we

ee - see three

ea – eat please

e_e - here

y – funny pretty

Book 19

Name _____

Read in 24 Lessons Ⓒ2019 Birthright Linda Wilson *lw*

1   Pretty please, may we
eat here?

2 Mom said she can meet
us here. Dad said he can
be here too.

3 I see them. Mom, Dad
and me makes three.

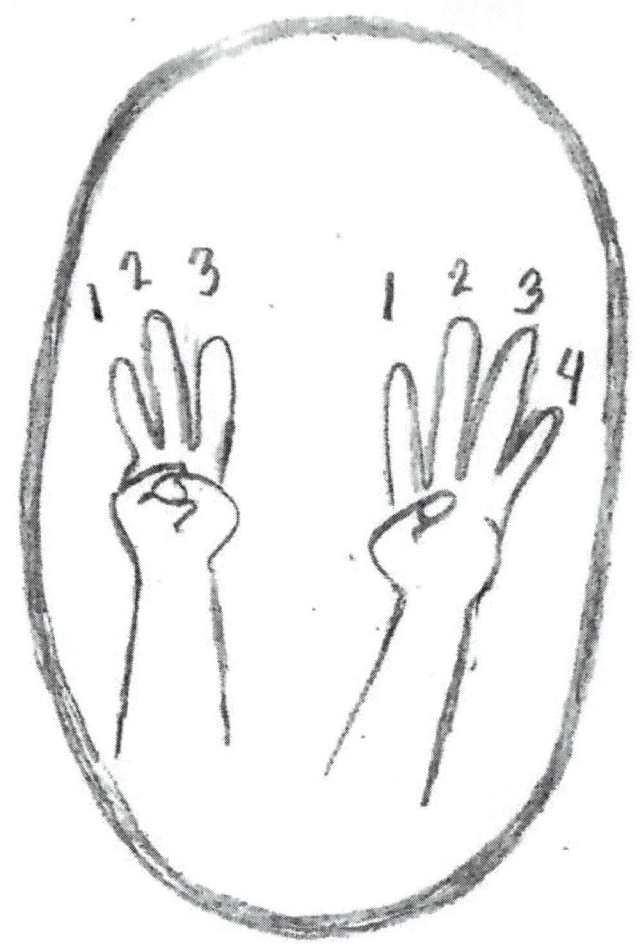

4 One more, you, makes
four.

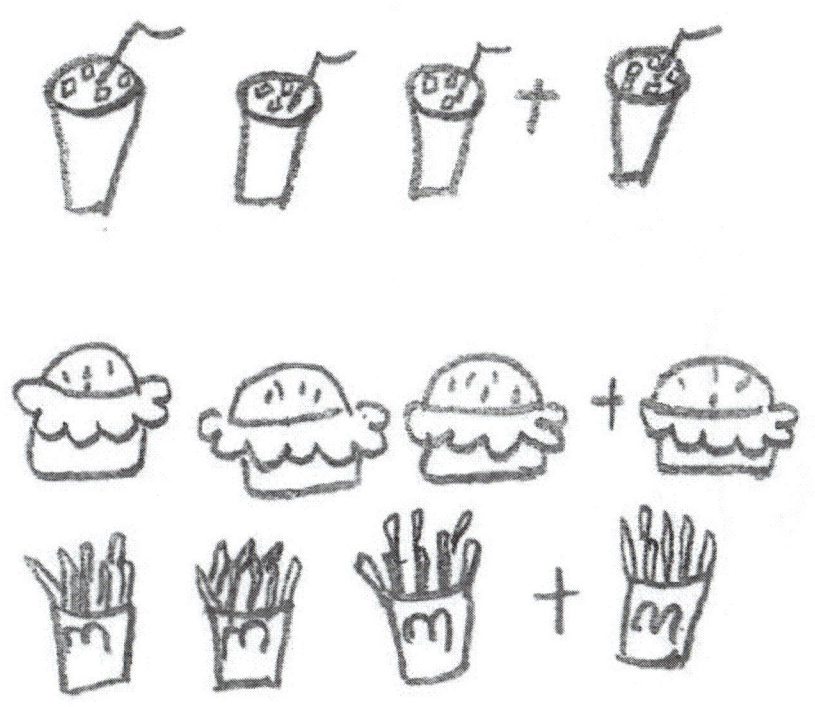

5   Is that funny? Yes!

6 The four of us can eat.

Yum, yum, yummy.

Dolch Pre-Primer Words

a and away big can come for <u>funny</u> go help **here** I in is it jump little make **me** my not one play red run said **see** the **three** to up **we** where

Remaining Pre-Primer Words

blue down find look two yellow you

7   **We are doing great!**
    Keep reading AR books!

Dolch Primer Words Book 19

all am are at ate **be** but
black came did do **eat**
four get have **he** into must
no on **please** pretty ran
saw say she so that there
they this too under want
was well went who with yes

Remaining Primer Words

brown good like new now
our out ride soon white

Keep reading AR books!

Sounding and Color Words

Traditionally, in public school, the first group of words to learn is the color words. Now, in Book 19, almost at the end of this reading series, we are talking about them. Why?

As you can see from the chart, the color words have a lot of vowel and consonant variations. The only way to teach so many different skills to a beginning reader is to not teach them at all. It is easier to just have the young reader memorize them.

I believe it is unfair not to teach the reading sounds and patterns of each new word. Your child is now fluent in sounding and phonics. It is time for the color words.

We have 6 books left. In 24 lessons, your child has been given a full set of reading skills.

A lifetime of reading success awaits your child.

Color Words – red yellow blue green purple orange brown white black tan pink gray

<u>short a</u> <u>long a</u> <u>short e</u> <u>long e</u>

tan   gray   red   green

black   yellow

orange (**ge** says j)

<u>short i</u>   <u>long i</u>   <u>short o</u>   <u>long o</u>

pink   white   yellow

<u>short u</u> <u>long u</u> <u>R vowels</u>

blue   orange purple

Consonant Digraph – **wh**ite

Vowel Diphthong – br**ow**n   10

Blends – **gr**ay **bl**ue **br**own

green black pink

be _____

he _____

me _____

she _____

we _____

see _____

three _____

eat _____

please _____

here _____

funny _____

pretty _____

Long Ii find like ride white (quiet e)

Book 20

Name _____

Read in 24 Lessons ℗2019 Birthright Linda Wilson ℒ𝓌

1 I can not find my

white hat.

2   I will ride my bike
to hunt for it.

3 There it is. I see my
pretty white hat.

4 Dad, do you like my hat ?

Yes, Mom, I like it a lot.

Dolch Pre-Primer Words

a and away big can
come **find** for funny
go help here I in is it
jump little make me
my not one play red
run said see the three
to up we where

Remaining Words

blue down look two
yellow you

Read AR Library Books

Dolch Primer Words Book 20

all am are at ate black
be but came did do
eat for get have he into
like must no please pretty
ride saw say she so that
there they this too under
want was well went what
white who will with yes

Remaining Words

brown good new now our
out soon

find _____

like _____

ride _____

white _____

find kind grind

like bike Mike

ride side hide

white bite kite

Long Vowel Oo

<u>yell**ow**</u> (quiet w)

Review n**o** s**o** g**o**

Introduce

Long Vowel Uu

<u>bl**ue**</u> (quiet e)

<u>Book 21</u>

Name_____

Read in 24 Lessons ©2019 Birthright Linda Wilson

1 What colors do I like?
I like yellow, blue,
and green.

2. What colors do you
like? You like blue
and gray.

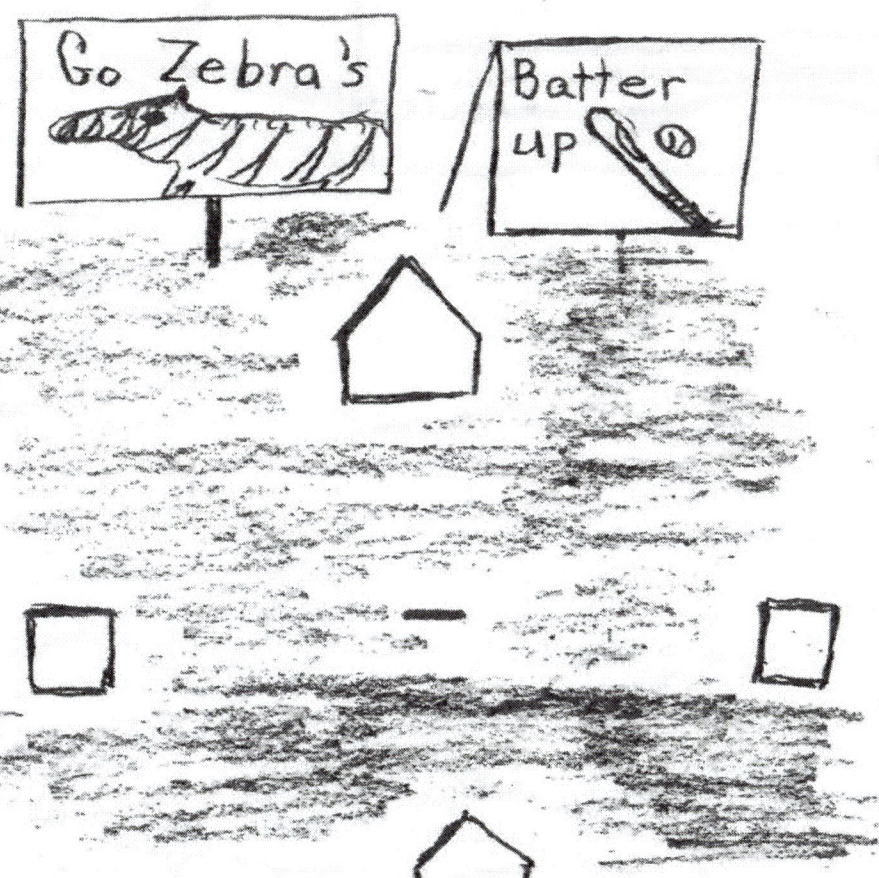

3 What colors do we
like? We like brown,
black and white.

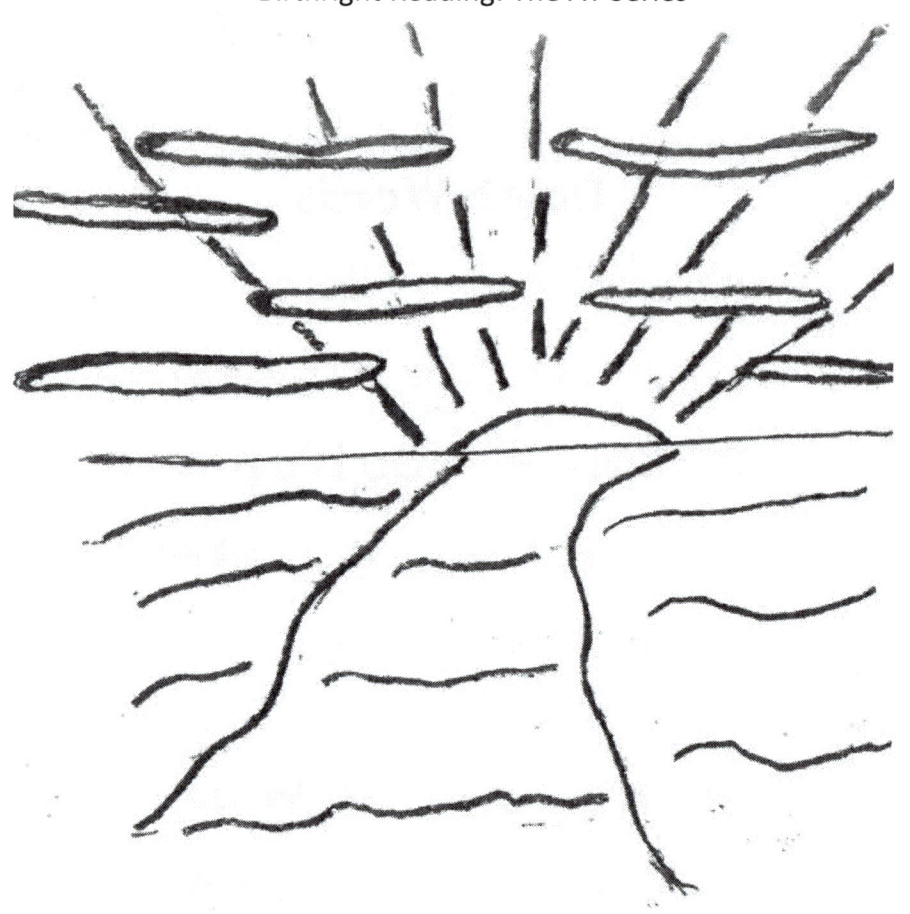

4. What colors do they like? They like orange, pink, red and purple.

Dolch Words

New Word - **yellow**

(short vowel **e** long **ow**)

Introduce – y**ou** bl**ue**

(ou and ue sound alike)

Introduce – br**ow**n

(**ow**-sounds like cow-It is not long o.)

Remaining Dolch Words

Pre-Primer – down look

two you blue

Primer - good new our

now out soon brown

Word Wall <u>Long Vowel</u> Review

It is up to the teacher and the students if you
want to have word wall words for long vowels.

ake – <u>make</u> take wake bake

rake lake cake Jake

ay – <u>away</u> <u>play</u> say day way

May Kay pay Ray Jay stay gray

ea – <u>eat</u> read seat cream

ee - <u>see</u> tree bee meet feet

ike- <u>like</u> Mike bike hike

ide – <u>ride</u> side slide wide hide

ow – <u>yellow</u> row low mow snow

show glow grow blow know

ue – <u>blue</u> glue Sue clue due

yell<u>ow</u> _____

sn**ow** _____

bl**ow** _____

gr**ow** _____

gl**ow** _____

sh**ow** _____

kn**ow** _____

l**ow** _____

m**ow** _____

r**ow** _____

cr**ow** _____

Long Vowel Uu

blue

Vowel Digraphs

Sounds Like Long Uu

soon two new you

Vowel Digraph

New Sound

look   good

Name _____

Book 22

1 I am blue. I miss you.
I hope to see you
soon.

2 Look! The two of us can

get a new car. Good!

We can get it! Yes, Yes!

3 We will go in the car and

look for a new cook book.

4. I have a good pal in you.

Having a new car and a new

cook book is what we need.

Book 22 Pre-Primer Words

a and away big **blue** can come find for funny go help here I in is it jump little **look** make me my not one play red run said see the three <u>to</u> **two** up we where yellow **you**

Remaining Word - down

Continue to read AR library books. You will love the last two lessons. I am proud of you.

Book 22 Dolch Primer Words

all am are at ate be
black but came did do
eat four get **good** have
he into like must **new** no
on please pretty ran ride
saw say she so **soon** that
there they this <u>too</u> under
want was well went what
white <u>who</u> will with yes

Words Remaining

brown now our out

blue _____

soon _____

two _____

new _____

you _____

New Sound

good _____

look _____

Read in 24 Lessons-Wilson

Birthright Reading ©2019 𝓛𝓦

Vowel Diphthongs

down brown now

our out

Vowel Diphthongs

oil boy Floyd

Book 23

43 Sounds Chart Included

Name _____

Read in 24 Lessons ©2019 Linda L. Wilson ℒ𝓌

ou-ow and oi-oy has two vowel sounds

1 Can we go down to the
ball park? Yes! Our car has
gas and oil. We can go now.

2 I will root for the Reds.

I will root for the Browns.

We can sing, "Take Me

Out to the Ball Game!"

3 I see Floyd. We can sit with him.

Go Reds! Go Browns!

<u>43</u> Speaking & Reading Sounds

<u>20 Consonant Sounds</u> – b c d

f g h j k l m n p q r s t v w x y z

c&k-same sound ph-says f gn-says n

s-can say z wr-says r q-needs u

ce ci cy say s   dge ge gi gy all say j

<u>5 Short Vowels</u> <u>a</u>t <u>e</u>gg <u>i</u>n <u>o</u>n <u>u</u>p

<u>5 Long Vowels</u> <u>a</u> b<u>e</u> <u>i</u>ce <u>o</u>h yo<u>u</u>

ai ay ea ee ie oa oe ow ue & quiet e

<u>3 Vowel Digraphs</u> 1 t<u>oo</u> n<u>ew</u>

2 <u>Au</u>gust s<u>aw</u> 3 l<u>oo</u>k g<u>oo</u>d

<u>5 Consonant Digraphs</u>

1<u>ch</u>ick 2<u>sh</u>e 3<u>th</u>e 4wi<u>th</u> 5<u>wh</u>ite

<u>3 R Vowels</u> 1 <u>ar</u>e 2 h<u>er</u> s<u>ir</u> f<u>ur</u> 3 f<u>or</u>

<u>2 Vowel Diphthongs</u> 1 ou/ow 2 oi/oy

1   <u>ou</u>t <u>ou</u>ch-<u>ow</u>l c<u>ow</u>

2   <u>oi</u>l s<u>oi</u>l-b<u>oy</u> t<u>oy</u>

Book 23 Dolch Pre-Primer Words

a and away big blue

can come **down** find

for funny go help here

I in is it jump little look

make me my not one

play red run said see

the three to two up we

where yellow you

We can read all 40 of

the Pre-Primer words.

Read Library AR Books!

Book 23 All of the Dolch Primer Words

all am are at ate be black brown but came did do eat four get good have he into like must new no now on our out please pretty ran ride saw say the so soon that there they this too under want was well went what white who will with yes

We know all 52 of the Dolch Primer words. Way to go!

down _____

brown _____

now _____

out _____

our _____

oil _____

boy _____

Floyd _____

Birthright Reading

Suggested AR Library Books

Books by P. D. Eastman

Fred and Ted Go Camping

Go Dog Go

Are You My Mother?

Big Dog Little Dog

Books by Mercer Mayer

Just Helping My Dad

All By Myself   Me Too

Books by James Dean

Pete the Cat

Too Cool for School

Pete at the Beach

Book 24

Oq(quack) Xx (fix next six)
Zz (Zebra Zippy please=z)

1 Zippy Bear is a vet. He likes to help and fix things.

2 One day, Quack the Duck came to see him. Zippy fixed Quack's leg.

3 The next day he saw two
zebras. They needed glasses.

4 Then, three dogs came
to him. He gave the sick
dogs each a shot.

5 Four cats came to see
him. Zippy helped them
find their way home.

6 Zippy looked at the clock. It was five o'clock. It was time to go home.

7 On his way home, he saw six blue birds. He gave them bird seed.

8 Zippy did not get home
until seven o'clock. He
ate fast and went outside.

9 Zippy mowed his lawn
until eight o'clock.

10 At nine o'clock,

Zippy got ready for bed.

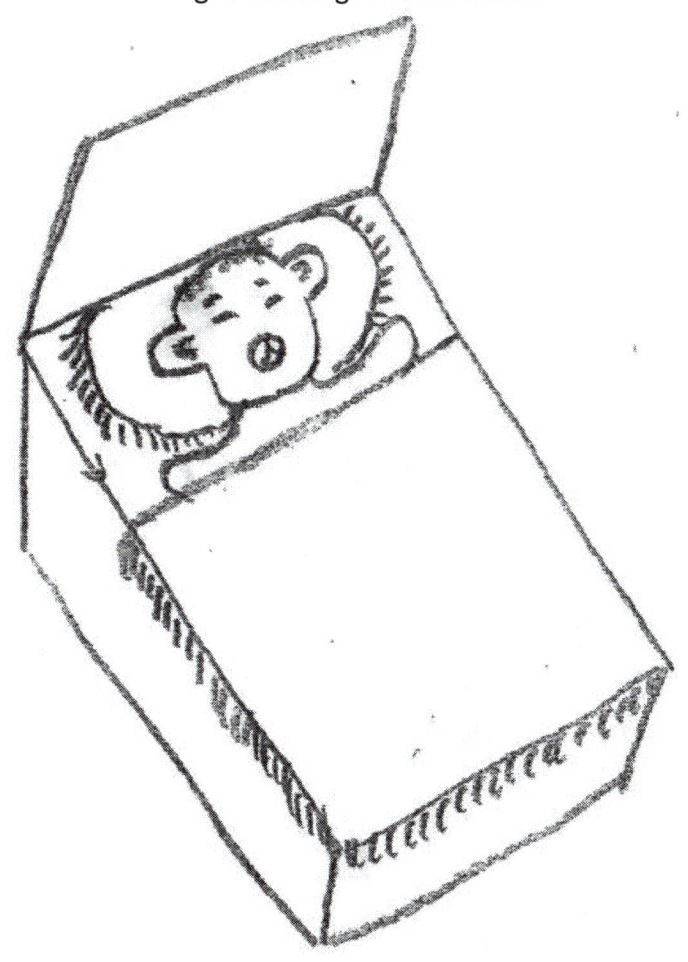

11 At ten o'clock Zippy was asleep. What will Zippy do next? He will help his pals.

Comprehension Questions

Who is Zippy? _____

Who did Zippy help?

_____

Where did he go at five?

_____

When did he go to sleep?

_____

Word Wall-Number Words

The number words, like the color words, are a group of words kindergarten students often memorize. There is no need to memorize them: We can easily sound them. However, two of the words, one and eight, must be memorized. One sounds like **wun** and eight sounds like **ate**.

short e   short i   short u

ten   six   one (memorize)

seven

long a   long e   long i

eight   three   five

(memorize)   nine

R Vowel - four

Vowel Digraph – two

Aa Bb Cc Dd Ee Ff Gg Hh Ii

Jj Kk Ll Mm Nn Oo Pp **Qq** Rr

Ss Tt Uu VvWw **Xx** Yy **Zz**

The Dolch Words don't have Qq, Xx, or Zz.

The kindergarten curriculum requires them.

Word Wall Words

Qq - a-quack i- quick

e- queen

Xx - a-ax fax Max

i – six fix mix   o – fox box

Zz - zebra Zippy zoom

please – se says z

You've finished the lessons!

Suggested AR Library Books

<u>Books by Alyssa Capucilli</u>

Biscuit Wins a Prize

Biscuit's New Trick

Biscuit Visits the Big City

Bath Time for Biscuit

<u>Books by Dr Seuss</u>

The Foot Book

The Eye Book

Great Day for Up

Marvin K. Mooney

Ten Apples on Top

Green Eggs and Ham

Hop on Pop

Name _____

Read in 24 Lessons Birthright ©2019 Wilson *LWJ*

After I retired, I ordered <u>Problems in Reading</u> by Edward Dolch. I wanted to see his original word lists. It was out-of-print in America. It arrived from India. I had to wait over a month on the book.

Think about it, I have a Masters Degree in Curriculum Development. I was never introduced to the cornerstone of reading. Most teachers believe Dolch intended for his word lists to be memorized, but that is totally false. Please sound all Dolch word lists, Pre-K – 4th grade.

After reading his book, it seemed clear that Dolch did not join the "whole-word-memorize" movement. Parents should know the American tradition of teaching reading with phonics that started with Noah Webster in 1824 and his <u>Blue Black Speller</u> still continues to be the best way to teach reading. Sounding works!

Our Constitution is based on God's Natural Laws. Teaching reading by memorizing words omits Natural Law. When a baby bear is born, he doesn't become an adult bear the next day. Memorizing words ignores the growth cycle of language and speech. Phonics and sounding recognize language progression. I pray that sounding instruction returns to our homes, public-schools, and universities. To God be the Glory!

Made in the USA
Columbia, SC
16 February 2021